the CHINESE *Secrets for* SUCCESS

the CHINESE *Secrets* for SUCCESS

FIVE INSPIRING CONFUCIAN VALUES

YUKONG ZHAO

NEW YORK

the CHINESE *Secrets for* SUCCESS
FIVE INSPIRING CONFUCIAN VALUES

ISBN 978-1-61448-535-3 paperback
ISBN 978-1-61448-536-0 eBook
ISBN 978-1-61448-537-7 Audio
Library of Congress Control Number: 2012956353

Morgan James Publishing
The Entrepreneurial Publisher
5 Penn Plaza, 23rd Floor,
New York City, New York 10001
(212) 655-5470 office • (516) 908-4496 fax
www.MorganJamesPublishing.com

Interior Design by:
Bonnie Bushman
bonnie@caboodlegraphics.com

DEDICATION

For Hubert and Selena.

TABLE OF CONTENTS

三人行，必有我师焉。

孔子

Whenever walking in a company of three, I will surely find someone I can learn from.

—Confucius

INTRODUCTION

I WROTE THIS BOOK for people who have a dream to provide a happy and prosperous life for their families. I wrote it especially for the many Americans who, like me, believe in "American Exceptionalism," but also recognize that their lives can be further improved by learning from the strengths of other cultures. More specifically, as a Chinese American, I wrote it to offer inspiration and proven solutions drawn from my cultural heritage to Americans seeking ways to deal with the tough challenges in their lives: impact of the financial crisis, rising global competition, decline of American education, and lack of financial security.

As we enter the 21st century, the most often discussed topic in the international arena is "the Rise of China." Since 1980, China has achieved a double digit economic growth rate and increased its economy by more than 15 times while the US has expanded its economy by only 1.3 times.[1,2] In 2010, China surpassed Japan to become the second largest economy in the world, next to the US. It is projected that, at this rate, the size of the Chinese economy will surpass that of the US before 2030.[3]

In addition to being the "world's factory" for manufacturing, China has become one of the leading nations in many high-tech areas, such as space technology, new energy development, and high-speed rail. According to a 2009 global education assessment report released by the Organization for Economic Cooperation and Development (OECD), 15-year-old kids in Shanghai, China are ranked #1 in reading, math, and science while the US now ranks 25th in math, 17th in science, and 14th in reading out of the 34 OECD countries.[4] Clearly, China is progressing faster than the US in many important aspects.

Let's go back a few decades, to the 1980s. Korea, Taiwan, Hong Kong, and Singapore, the so-called "Four Asian Mini-Dragons," achieved rapid economic growth and became newly industrialized countries. Two decades earlier, in the 1960s, Japan recovered from the ruins of World War II, rapidly grew its economy, and became a major global economic power.

Economically speaking, what do these countries have in common? They started with poor economic conditions and rapidly grew into economic powers of the world. Culturally speaking, what do these countries have in common? All of them are Asian countries influenced by Confucian values. What does this tell us?

In 1979, Herman Kahn, the world-famous futurist, pointed out the cultural strengths of the Confucian Ethic in the pursuits of industrialization and affluence.[5] In 1980, Roderick MacFarquhar, the world-renowned China expert and former Director of the John King Fairbank Center for East Asian Research at Harvard University, attributed the rapid economic growth of Japan and the "Four Asian Mini-Dragons" to the Confucian Ethic.[6] Both of them wisely predicted the rise of East Asian economies 30 years ago.

If we turn now to the people, Chinese Americans, along with Japanese Americans, Korean Americans, and a few other Asian American ethnic groups, have been recognized as "the Model Minority" by the American media since 1960s. In the Pew Research Center Report "The Rise of

Asian Americans" of June 19, 2012, Asian Americans are applauded as "the highest-income, best-educated, and fastest-growing racial group in the US."[7] They are among the leading ethnic groups in achieving "the American Dream" of getting a high-quality education, having a good job, and making a prosperous living. Following are a few impressive facts with regard to Asian Americans and Chinese Americans (you can find more details in Chapter 2):

1. Family income: In 2009, the median income of Asian Americans was $68,780 while for Chinese Americans it was $69,502. At the same time the median income of the U.S. population in general was $50,221.[8]

2. Education: In 2010, 49% of Asian Americans and 51.1% of Chinese Americans held a college degree or higher while the percentage for the general American population was only 28.2%.[9] Over 90% of Asian American high school graduates enrolled in college[10]. Their enrollment in the most prestigious universities in America, including the Ivy League schools, UC Berkeley, Stanford, and MIT, is several times higher than their 5.6% as reflected in the U.S. population.[11]

3. Family management and crime control: Asian Americans generally have lower rates of divorce, obesity, crime, and drug abuse than the general population. For example, the divorce rate among Asian Americans is less than half of the national average and the crime rate is only one quarter of the national average.[12]

Today, the majority of Chinese Americans work in science, engineering, education, and business arenas. They are among the key contributors to the technology innovation of the US and have made remarkable achievements in many areas and even include seven Nobel laureates.

Another thing that makes Asian and Chinese Americans stand out is their ability to survive the financial crisis of 2008.[13] With higher educational levels, the unemployment rate is lower for them. With good money management skills, they were able to fend off greedy lenders and had fewer foreclosures. Although most of them are not wealthy, with a well-established practice of saving, many of them were able to buy houses as an investment when the prices hit rock bottom in 2009 and 2010.

Very importantly, Asian and Chinese Americans succeed in many critical areas that our nation is struggling, such as science and math education, money management, family stability, crime and obesity control.

What are the secrets of success for Chinese Americans? Again, they are the many inspiring Confucian values that have been influencing China and other East Asian countries for more than two thousand years. After the Chinese emigrated to the US, they embraced and benefited from many important Western values such as rule of law, equal rights, and independent thinking. At the same time, they retained much of their own cultural heritage, predominantly Confucian values, such as the emphasis on education, saving, and devotion to the family. It is the combination of positive values drawn from both Confucianism and Western culture that make many Chinese/Asian Americans successful in their pursuit of the American Dream!

For many decades, despite many publications by Herman Kahn, Roderick MacFarquhar, Tu Weiming, and other scholars on China/East Asia, these success secrets largely have been confined to the academic world. Most mainstream readers outside Asian societies do not know these inspiring Confucian values and thus are unable to reap the benefits from them.

As an ethnic Chinese who grew up in China, I was deeply influenced by Confucian values since childhood. In particular, after Deng Xiaoping initiated the Open and Reform Policy in the late 1970s, I witnessed the powerful release of the cultural energy of Confucian values that has been driving the country from poverty to prosperity. In 1992, I moved to the US and became a member of the Asian American community. During my stay in the US, I have observed that a lot of

Chinese Americans who apply Confucian values in their lives bring success to themselves and their families.

In this book, I'd like to share with you the key Confucian values that remain enlightening and beneficial in modern society. Importantly, I will share with you how Chinese Americans apply such values to their lives in helping them to pursue the American Dream. You will discover, in the pages that follow, that while many Confucian values and principles are easy to understand, it is the implementation of them that makes the difference.

This book is organized into two parts and eight chapters.

Part I. Why Does America Need Confucian Values? It consists of three chapters:

- Using broad social and economic data as a foundation, Chapter 1 strategically analyzes the key challenges facing the US: global competition, decline in education quality, skyrocketing government debt, the looming insolvency of Social Security and Medicare, and high oil prices. It reveals an unpleasant truth: Since the financial crisis, the US has entered a challenging time. In order to maintain a good living standard, many Americans need to change their lifestyles and the ways they parent their children.

- Based on compelling data, both historical and recent, Chapter 2 illustrates the far-ranging influences that Confucian values have created in ancient China, the rapid economic growth of Japan, Taiwan, Korea, Singapore, Hong Kong, and the rise of China, as well as the extraordinary achievements made by Chinese Americans and Asian Americans as "the Model Minority" in the US. It points out that often the secrets behind these success stories are inspiring Confucian values.

- Chapter 3 introduces the five inspiring Confucian values that are positively influencing today's Chinese society. This chapter will briefly introduce the origin of Confucian philosophy, its evolution throughout history, and how Chinese people adapt it usefully into secular living guidelines, making them highly competitive in modern society.

In Part II. The Five Inspiring Confucian Values, I will use chapters 4 through 8 to discuss each Confucian value in great detail. Each chapter starts with a review of why a Confucian value is important to today's American society. It then introduces the Confucian values and principles in this subject area. Following that, each chapter will describe how Chinese people apply Confucian values to their daily lives to make them successful. From many examples, you will find out how Confucianism-influenced Chinese families set up career and educational objectives, parent their children, make money management decisions, and handle family and friendship issues. At the end of chapters 5 and 7, I will discuss how to strike a balance between good Confucian values and Western values so you can utilize the strengths from both sides simultaneously. For readers who already have a good understanding of the benefits of Confucian values but are eager to learn the principles and how to apply these five Confucian values, they may quickly scan through the first three chapters (Part I) and focus on Part II of this book.

Part II consists of five chapters:

- Chapter 4 will discuss the First Confucian Value: *Li-zhi* (立志) "Determination for an Outstanding Life." It first talks about the need to have a big dream for yourself and in particular for your children. It then introduces the Confucian value of *li-zhi* and discloses the secret of how Confucianism-influenced Chinese families use *li-zhi* to create motivation and build personal character in order to achieve outstanding life objectives.

- Chapter 5 will cover the Second Confucian Value: *Qin-xue* (勤学) "Pursuing an Excellent Education." Education is China's "national passion" and the main vehicle for the Chinese to achieve career and life objectives. In this chapter, I will share with you the origin of this value, how the Chinese people respect knowledge and emphasize education, and more importantly, how they apply Confucian educational methods to achieve outstanding educational goals for their children.

- Chapter 6 will focus on the Confucian way of money management, the Third Confucian Value: *Jie-jian* (节俭) "Saving for a Better Life." Beginning with how important money management is in the US, this chapter will share with you how to use Confucian values and principles to make wise money management decisions. It will explain how, although most Chinese Americans are reputable for their money-saving habits, they also spend money on name brand cars and live in desirable neighborhoods. How can Chinese American families achieve this while other families with similar incomes cannot?

- Chapter 7 will introduce the Fourth Confucian Value: *Gu-jia* (顾家) "Caring for Your Family," which is one of the core values of Confucian philosophy. Besides discussing the benefits and approaches to maintaining a stable and loving family, it will teach you how to use *qi-jia* (齐家), a key Confucian value, to help you to manage your family successfully: to avoid undesirable family risks, facilitate career development, and achieve good health, happiness, and other family goals.

- And finally, in Chapter 8, I will illustrate the Fifth Confucian Value: *Ze-you* (择友) "Developing Desirable Friendships." This chapter will share with you many rich Confucian values on how to build successful interpersonal relationships, how to avoid bad influences and select desirable friends who can benefit your life and your career, and how to choose a desirable neighborhood that could help shape the future of your children.

These five Confucian values provide readers with insightful guidance on many essential areas of life. They cover setting up career aspirations and building personal character (*li-zhi*), education for your career and life skill development (*qin-xue*), money management skills (*jie-jian*), family management and parenting (*gu-jia*), and selecting and developing beneficial relationships (*ze-you*).

In the latter part of the 17th century, one of great thinkers and philosophers, Gottfried Leibniz, predicted, "As the most cultivated and distant peoples (Europe and China) stretch out their arms to each other, those in between may gradually be brought to a better way of life."[14] This is exactly what is happening to Confucianism-influenced Chinese/Asian Americans who benefit from the strengths of both cultures. The same can happen to many people from other cultural/ethnical backgrounds, if they are open-minded to oriental wisdom!

I'd like to point out here that the premise and main approach I used in this book is called "best practice sharing," which is widely used in corporate America and many multinational companies. In this approach, Company A tries to identify and learn the specific areas in which Company B excels, even though Company A may be overall better than Company B. In learning from the strengths of Company B, Company A is able to continuously improve itself, which is essential for Company A to thrive in the competitive business world. I introduce the inspiring Confucian values to people of different cultures because I see the strengths of Confucian values in these areas. There is no intent to imply that, in general, Western culture or any other culture is not as good as Confucianism-oriented cultures. It is Western culture that has played a leading role in establishing modern political and market systems. Confucianism, on the other hand, has illustrated its lasting values in personal and family development. In such areas as education and family management, I see the strengths of both Confucian and Western approaches so I advise readers to take an approach that combines the advantages of both so optimal results can be achieved.

Obviously, every ethnic group has its successful families/people and good values that can be usefully adopted by other ethnic groups. Americans are admired for their spirit of freedom and creativity. Jews rank among the highest achievers in the fields of science and business management. Germans are well known for their engineering strength. Chinese Americans, along with Japanese and Korean Americans, are good practitioners of inspiring Confucian values, which have helped them to become the recognized "Model Minority" in the US. By opening our minds to the worthwhile cultural values of other societies—Confucian, Jewish, German, Indian, Finish, French, and more—I sincerely hope it will also generate American interest in rediscovering the values that make America successful. When good values and practices are promoted, society will reap the benefits and the country will advance.

Finally, I'd like to emphasize that the focus of this book is not on making generalizations about race, but on sharing the inspiring values of Confucius, which have had a lasting impact on many races: Chinese, Korean, Japanese, and others. People benefit from learning from others. As Confucius put it, "Whenever walking in a company of three, I will surely find someone I can learn from (三人行，必有我师焉)."[15] Part of what made Confucius a great thinker was his open mind. Why can't we be the same way?

PART I.

Why Does America Need Confucian Values?

Chapter 1

CHALLENGING
TIMES ARE AHEAD

AT THE END OF the 20ᵗʰ century, the U.S. economy was booming and enjoyed one of the longest periods of economic expansion since World War II. American household incomes had increased. The Dow Jones and NASDAQ Indexes were rising. Real estate was appreciating. American productivity was up. It was a prosperous time. Americans were enjoying good lives: they moved to larger houses, bought larger automobiles, and spent more and more.

After entering the 21ˢᵗ century, however, the United States encountered a number of unprecedented economic and security setbacks: the boom and bust of the Internet and telecommunications industries, the Enron and WorldCom scandals, the September 11 terrorist attacks, and two costly wars, one in Afghanistan beginning in 2001 and the other in Iraq beginning in 2003. The combination of both wars has cost thousands of American lives and, as of February

2011, more than $1.369 trillion dollars in direct costs (not including indirect costs such as spending on veterans).[1]

Following that was a jump in oil prices, to a new high of $145 per barrel in July 2008.[2] At the end of 2008, the sub-prime mortgage bubble burst, and the US began its largest economic recession since the Great Depression of the 1930s.

From December 2007 to December 2009, the US lost 8.7 million jobs.[3] The unemployment rate reached a high of 10.2% in October 2009,[4] the highest point since the Great Depression. From 2008 to 2010, over 8 million homes received a foreclosure notice.[5] By 2011, 46.2 million Americans (about 15% of the U.S. population) were considered to be living in poverty.[6] In order to fight the economic recession, the George W. Bush and Obama Administrations launched bank bailouts, economic recovery programs, and other massive spending endeavors that drove the U.S. national debt to a new high of $16 trillion in 2012.[7] The US entered an economically difficult time.

Starting in 2011, the U.S. economy finally began to show signs of recovery. The unemployment rate dropped to 7.8% in September 2012.[8] Although virtually no one disagrees that the economy will recover down the road, many Americans started to ask: Does a U.S. recovery mean a return to the good old days? Can many Americans continue their way of spending beyond their means, living in larger and larger homes, and driving larger and larger automobiles?

Drawing on my twenty-plus years of experience in corporate strategic planning, I gathered the key facts that stand to impact the future of the US, and based on this conducted a strategic analysis. The results suggest a very challenging scenario: Although the US is still the number one economic and technological power in the world, many nations are rapidly catching up. Faced with a host of domestic and global challenges, many Americans may no longer be able to sustain the lifestyle they enjoyed in the last decade. In order to maintain a good quality of life, it is necessary that the American people and their leaders find ways to cope with economic and political challenges domestically and internationally. The situation calls for a bold change in policy by the government as well as a dramatic change in behavior by many American people. Let me tell you why…

1.1 INCREASING GLOBAL COMPETITION IS TAKING AWAY MANY MIDDLE CLASS JOBS FROM THE US

While international trade has existed for thousands of years, it was not until the second half of the 20th century that the globalization process sped up dramatically. After World War II, the General Agreement on Tariffs and Trade (GATT) was set up in 1948 to promote international trade. In 1995, the World Trade Organization (WTO) was established to replace GATT. With the efforts of GATT and now WTO, international trade barriers have been significantly reduced. The U.S. government has also signed a number of free trade agreements with various countries, such as the North American Free Trade Agreement (NAFTA) with Canada and Mexico in 1993. One direct impact of these trade agreements is that manufacturing jobs have moved from industrial nations such as the US to newly industrialized countries such as Japan, Korea, Taiwan in the 1970s and 1980s, and then to developing countries such as China and Mexico after the 1990s.

After U.S. manufacturing employment reached its peak of 19.55 million jobs in 1979, over the last three decades, the manufacturing sector has lost more than 40% of its workforce, almost 8 millions jobs. Unfortunately, the trend has been exacerbated by national and international developments since 2000. The US has lost 6 million jobs, 75% of the total, in just the last 10 years.[9]

While gains in productivity have partially contributed to the reduction of manufacturing jobs in the US, global competition is another major factor. It manifests in the loss of many manufacturing industries in the US. At first, the US lost the labor-intensive industries such as the apparel and textile industries, followed by a majority of its electronics industries, steel and fabrication industries, the furniture industry, and other industries. In recent years, many high-tech products such as computers and printers have been manufactured in China and other countries. What is the impact of such manufacturing job loss in the US? More and more Americans are forced to switch to low paid service jobs.

Unfortunately, with globalization this trend is going to continue. A good example is the auto industry. In the recent restructuring of GM, the union finally agreed to allow 40% of new plants to operate with wages set at $14/hour, which is equal to a salary of $35,000 per year, about $10,000 less than the U.S. median household income. Even after the manufacturing wage has been driven down so low, it still is not competitive globally. As a comparison, in GM's subsidiary in Mexico, workers earn only $7/hour.[10] As a result, many multinational companies cannot resist the allure of global sourcing: More and more jobs are being relocated to low-cost countries such as Mexico and Vietnam. In the meantime, countries like Japan, Korea, and China are nurturing their manufacturers, competing with American workers directly by exporting more goods into the US.

By early 2012, there were signs that some American companies had started to move manufacturing jobs back to the US. This trend, however, is still small, limited to a few bright spots in which the US has resources or other advantages. Considering the higher wages and higher corporate tax rates (as compared to emerging countries) as well as political uncertainty in the US, there is no compelling reason to believe that this small trend will grow into a big wave any time soon. In an NPR interview on March 13, 2012 Howard Hauser, vice president of Hiawatha Rubber Company, which moved some manufacturing jobs back to the US recently, said the future of U.S. manufacturing does not lay in bringing jobs back, but in improving productivity through increased automation, which will eventually reduce the manufacturing labor force.[11]

If we have seen a gloomy picture regarding the loss of the manufacturing jobs in the US, the ongoing loss of American service jobs is downright scary. The advancement of telecommunication and information technology, in particular the Internet, has created a borderless service platform. Service personnel in faraway countries now can provide a host of services to American customers: call centers, computer troubleshooting services, and many others. These kinds of jobs have been rapidly shifted to India, the Philippines, and other countries. Alan Blinder, a distinguished economist and Princeton professor, estimates that 28 million to 42 million American service jobs eventually will be "susceptible" to be outsourced to other countries.[12] If that is the case, the number of American service jobs being impacted will be far greater than the number of manufacturing jobs the US has lost in the last three decades.

1.2 DECLINING AMERICAN EDUCATIONAL COMPETITIVENESS IS ERODING MANY HIGH-PAID U.S. JOBS

If the loss of manufacturing and service jobs ultimately means the depletion of the American middle class whose members depend on such jobs to feed their families, another more dangerous trend is emerging: the gradual erosion of U.S. high-tech industries. After World War II, Europe and Japan rapidly developed their high-tech industries and have since become key players in this arena. In recent decades, China, Korea, Taiwan, Singapore, and other Asian countries "are quickly ascending as science and technology leaders, and our position will continue to decline without significant efforts to maintain and strengthen the U.S. innovation system, with major implications for our economic competitiveness, national security, and international leadership," according to a report released by the National Science Board in 2010.[13] Today, although the US still leads the world in many high-tech industries, its ability to sustain its leadership is in question because of its declining educational quality.

The same 2009 OECD report in which Shanghai, China was ranked No.1 across reading, science, and mathematics revealed a disappointing performance by U.S. students. Out of 34 OECD countries, 15-year-old American students ranked only 14th in reading (above average), 17th in science (about average), and 25th in mathematics (well below average), despite the fact U.S. funding for education is the second highest in the world.[14] These results were regarded as a wakeup call by the U.S. Secretary of Education, Arne Duncan. College education numbers are equally disappointing. The

US ranked only 12[15] in developed countries in college graduation rate.[15] Only 53% of American college students are able to graduate from a four-year college within six years.[16]

In the meantime, other countries are rapidly advancing their education systems. Today China has built the largest higher education system in the world, with annual college graduates numbering 5.6 million in 2008 alone, 42% of which obtained science, technology, engineering and mathematics (STEM) degrees This number is still growing. As a comparison, in 2008 the US had about 1.6 million college graduates, with only 14% of them earning a degree from STEM majors.[17] Even combined with graduates from Master's and doctoral degree programs, the US turnout is dwarfed by the total number of science and engineering graduates from China alone, not to mention those from Europe, Japan, Korea, Singapore, and other countries with high rates of educational achievement. As for the impact on the American quality of life: More and more highly paid research and development (R&D) jobs are being created outside the US, and more and more innovation jobs will follow. This concern is widely shared by political and business leaders such as Condoleezza Rice, Bill Gates, and many experts in the education arena, including Anthony Carnevale, Director of the Center on Education and the Workforce at Georgetown University.[18] If the US loses its technology leadership, there is little chance for most Americans to maintain their relatively high living standard. As President Obama put it, the nation that "out-educates us today will out-compete us tomorrow."[19]

Jobs are the primary source of income for most people. When more and more middle class and even high-paid jobs are being lost, it creates a detrimental impact on the economic wellbeing of today's Americans, and more importantly, on generations to come.

1.3 Skyrocketing U.S. Budget Deficit and National Debt Will Create a Burden on American Economies and Citizens Alike

The public debt of the US originated during the American revolutionary war. In the first 150 years of the nation, it rose during the Civil War and World War I and decreased when the country was at peace. The national debt was kept at a low level as the early administrations implemented disciplined surplus policies. The Great Depression, World War II, and the Cold War in the 1980s drove up the national debt substantially.[20] At the end of the last century, the Clinton Administration was able to run a budget surplus and held the gross public debt to $5.7 trillion accumulatively in January 2001. During the administration of President George W. Bush, the tax cut, along with the wars in Iraq and Afghanistan, accelerated the federal deficit. By the end of his administration in December 2008, the national debt had reached $10.7 trillion. Under President Barack Obama, with massive spending to stimulate the economy, the debt increased from $10.7 trillion to $16 trillion by August, 2012, which exceeds the size of the U.S. GDP, the total size of the economy.[21]

What is the outlook? According to the Congressional Budget Office in its 10-year budget and economic outlook update issued in August 2011, the US is going to add an additional $8.5 trillion of national debt over the next decade.[22]

What does such high national debt mean to the country and to American citizens?

- A high percentage of taxpayer money has to be used to make the interest payment. In 2008, the interest reached $454 billion, equal to 18% of the tax revenue. This means that for every tax dollar Uncle Sam collects, 18 cents goes to pay interest. In the next decade, it is estimated that $4.8 trillion will be spent on the interest payment alone.
- Higher borrowing costs and higher interest payments. After the national debt surpasses 100% of GDP, the risk of borrowing will become higher, as will the interest rate and payment.
- The pressure to cut spending on other needed investments such as U.S. education, R&D, and infrastructure as well as social benefits such as Medicare and Social Security.[23]

- Increased possibility to slow down economic growth, according to economic research conducted by Kenneth Rogoff and Carmen Reinhart in 2010.[24]
- If the government increases marginal tax rates significantly to pay the rising interest costs, people will have less savings and less incentive to work hard.

Due in large part to the mounting debt, the mid-term elections of 2010 elected many Tea Party members and fiscally conservative Republicans to Congress, shifting control of the House to the Republicans. At the top of their agenda: Cut federal government spending. Similarly, many state governments are faced with huge budget deficits. Their solutions are the same: Cut spending. The direct impact on Americans is quite serious: less government spending on social programs and investment. As individuals, many Americans will have to settle for reduced social benefits from the government, meaning they will have to depend more on themselves.

1.4 UNSUSTAINABLE SOCIAL SECURITY AND MEDICARE PROGRAMS WILL LEAD TO A POSTPONEMENT IN OR REDUCTION OF BENEFITS FOR AMERICAN RETIREES

At present, most American seniors depend on Social Security and Medicare as their key sources of income and healthcare insurance coverage. As of June 30, 2009, 51.9 million Americans, or 16.9% of the U.S. population, were receiving monthly Social Security benefits. As of 2010, Social Security paid an average of $22,704/year to retired couples and $13,968/year to retired individuals. This constitutes more than 50% of the income for 63% of American retirees.[25] About 45 million American seniors received Medicare benefits in 2008.[26] Medicare, in combination with Medicaid, provides essential healthcare support for American seniors and the poor. As a matter of fact, Social Security is the largest pension program and Medicare is the largest health insurance program in the US.

While both programs are still solvent today, their sustainability is challenged by two major factors: the aging American population and increasing obesity in the US.

For the US, the single most important demographic change in the early 21st century is the retirement of the post-World War II baby boomers. After successfully defeating Germany, Italy, and Japan, American GIs returned home and embarked on peaceful family lives, generating a period of high population growth. From 1946 to 1964, approximately 76 million babies were born, creating a U.S. population peak in the 20th century.[27] When the baby boomers reached working age, they helped to create unprecedented prosperity in the U.S. economy. When they start to retire, they will create an unprecedented surge in Medicare and Social Security payouts. With the extension of the life expectancy in the US, it is estimated that by 2030, the total enrollment will reach 78 million. This would represent more than a 50% increase from the current level. What does this mean for Social Security and Medicare? It means the ratio between contributors to these programs and recipients of benefits is decreasing. Take for example Medicare: Currently there are 3.9 persons paying tax into Medicare for every American receiving benefits. By 2030, when baby boomers fully retire, this ratio is projected to be reduced to 2.4.[28] Aging will significantly increase Social Security and Medicare spending.

In addition to aging, increasing obesity in the US will boost Medicare and Medicaid spending. Today, two-thirds of all adults and about a third of all children and teenagers in the US are either overweight or obese.[29] Even more alarming is the fact that 70% of obese adolescents will become obese adults.[30] According to a scientific estimate, the direct medical costs related to obesity in the US in 2008 were $147 billion a year.[31] A significant percentage of that cost is paid by Medicare and Medicaid. The unfortunate truth is this: The trend of obesity has yet to be brought under control.

The net result of these demographic and social changes is that neither Social Security nor Medicare is sustainable. According to the Social Security and Medicare Boards of Trustees 2011 Reports,[32] starting in 2010, Social Security is projected to spend more than it collects in taxes every year indefinitely. By 2036, Social Security funds will be exhausted and no more payments will be made to retirees if no sweeping reform is enacted beforehand. The situation for Medicare is even more dire. The report projects that federal Medicare costs will rise from 3.6% of GDP in 2010 to 5.5% in 2035. The Medicare hospital insurance fund will become insolvent by 2024, five years earlier than their estimate made in 2010.

At present, leaders from both parties realize the urgent need to reform Social Security and Medicare. Sooner or later it will come. The only question is whether Social Security and Medicare benefits are to be delayed or reduced. What will the impact be on working or younger Americans? They will need to work harder and save more for their retirement.

1.5 Likelihood of a Return to the Era of High Oil Prices After the Global Economic Recession

With 5% of the world's population, the US consumes 22% of the world's oil supply or about 18.8 million barrels per day. The next biggest oil consumer, China, with a population more than four times that of the US, consumes only 8.3 million barrels per day.[33] Each year, the average U.S. motorist drives about 13,000 miles[34] and consumes about 550 gallons of gasoline.[35] When the price was about $2 per gallon, it added up to $1,100 per passenger car. When the price increased to $4 per gallon in 2007, on average each American driver paid $2,200 per year for gasoline. High oil prices create a significant financial burden on most Americans.

With the economic recession, the price of gasoline dropped back to $2 per gallon at the end of November 2008. But it rose to $3.5 per gallon at the end of October 2012. The question is: Will the price of gasoline stay at a low level (less than $2.50 per gallon) after the economic recession is over? The answer is: It is very unlikely. Here are the reasons:

At first, the economic growth emerging economies such as China and India will continue to drive up oil demand. Represented by so called "Golden BRIC" nations, including Brazil, Russia, India, and China, a number of developing countries have sustained rapid economic growth in recent years/decades. This drives an improvement of the living standard and ownership of personal automobiles, which translates directly into a rapid increase in oil demand. From 2006 to 2010, China had an annual growth of automobile sales of 9.51 million, reaching the 100 million mark by September 2011.[36] With economic growth and more purchasing power, more and more Chinese people will buy automobiles, which will directly lead to a continuous increase in oil demand. Similar economic growth is driving up the ownership of automobiles in India, South Africa, and other emerging economies.

Secondly, the production and supply of the world's oil has become increasingly difficult and costly.[37] In the 20th and previous centuries, oil producers had the luxury to explore and produce oil from reserves that were relatively easy to tap. Since most of the easily tapped oil reserves have been exploited, oil producers have to rely on more complicated methods such as the injection of water, air, and chemicals into the ground to get the oil out. This means higher production costs. More importantly, oil producers now have to move to more geologically challenging places to exploit oil, such as the deep sea and very remote deserts. Again, this leads to significant cost increases. The foremost thing to keep in mind about oil is that it is a fossil-based energy resource that is not renewable. Human beings have only about 60 years of reserves left to exploit. It will become more and more costly to produce the same barrel of oil even given the same level of production. The increasing world demand for oil will drive the price even higher.

On top of the production cost increase, supply instability has also created a significant risk around the world's oil supply. Any geopolitical conflict in an oil-producing region could significantly increase the price of oil, such as the recent war in Iraq and the Iraq and Iran war during the 1980s. Any natural disaster or political risk on the transportation path, by sea, land, or pipeline, will also disrupt supply, driving up the price of oil. Unfortunately, this kind of disruption may happen at any time, in particular political risks, as we have seen over the last century.

This is because most oil-producing regions, in particular the Middle East and Africa, as of yet have no stable political systems in place. The demonstrations in Tunisia, Egypt, Bahrain, Yemen, and Libya in the spring of 2011 stand as vivid examples. They drove up the average price of gasoline in the US from around $3.00 per gallon to $3.50 per gallon in just a few weeks.

In the non-conventional oil & gas sector, however, we do have some good news. In the late 1990's, Mitchell Energy, a US company, led the technological breakthrough called hydraulic fracturing on shale gas exploration and production. As a result, the US has significantly increased natural gas production and driven down its prices. After more and more countries adopt this technology, natural gas will become an important energy substitute to oil in some applications, resulting a slow down of the rise of oil prices in the future. Nevertheless, oil prices will still grow in the next two decades because of reasons we discussed above. According to "Annual Energy Outlook 2012," released by the US Department of Energy, from 2012 to 2035, oil prices will likely grow from $100 to $150 per barrel.[38]

If we combine the major factors that influence oil price, we are forced to draw an uncomfortable conclusion: Oil prices will return to what they were during the high-price era. It is very unlikely that we will see a price of $40 or lower per barrel sustainable in the future. What will be the impact on American consumers? High driving costs down the road.

These five key trends entail undeniable forces in today's America and the world that are driving down Americans' competitiveness and their quality of life. It is an unfortunate truth that has been awakening Americans every day. According to a September 2010 *Newsweek* poll, 63% of Americans said they did not think they would be able to maintain their current standard of living.[39] International competition and domestic issues have combined to negatively impact a large number of Americans. They will, sooner or later, be forced to change their lifestyles. They have to make change the way they handle life and career, manage money and family, and more importantly, educate their children to become more competitive.

Chapter 2.

THE BENEFITS OF CONFUCIAN INFLUENCE

2.1 WHY DOES AMERICA NEED TO LEARN FROM OTHER CULTURES?

Throughout human history, cultures have emerged and disappeared, such as the Maya; some have survived but continue to struggle, such as many of the poor nations in Africa; some progress assertively, such as Western industrial nations and Asian newly industrialized countries. What are the reasons behind such disparate modes of development? Might they have anything to do with cultural values?

Max Weber, a great thinker and one of the founders of modern sociology, analyzed the rise of capitalism in 1904, when he drew an insightful conclusion in his famous essay, "The Protestant Ethic and the Spirit of Capitalism."[1] The rise of capitalism, bureaucracy, and the rational-legal nation-state, he wrote, can be attributed to ascetic

Protestantism. It is a great example of how cultural values can help promote the civilization of society. Clearly, good cultural values help a culture/nation to survive and prosper. Human societies advance when they create or adopt good cultural values.

Today, the essence of modern Western civilization is still vibrant. It includes the free market system, the democratic political system, and the rule of law. Nevertheless, as we embark on the 21st century we are faced with huge challenges: increasing global competition, declining U.S. educational competitiveness, skyrocketing national and personal debt, unsustainable Social Security and Medicare systems, and looming high oil prices. Under these conditions, an open-minded person may ask: Are there any other cultural values we can learn to help us sustain our prosperity and improve our lives and those of our younger generation?

The answer is yes. Although the US still maintains its global competitive edge, other nations are progressing at a faster pace, rapidly closing the gap. We can learn from the cultural values of such nations. As an immigration country, the US has attracted immigrants from various cultures. Some ethnic groups are faring significantly better than average. We can also learn something from these ethnic groups. It is this kind of open-minded attitude that has made the United States a world leader. It will also take this kind of open-minded attitude for us to sustain our prosperity and improve our lives!

2.2 THE CHINESE AND ASIAN SUCCESSES AND THEIR UNTOLD SECRETS

Why do we need to learn from Confucian values? Do people benefit from Confucian values? After studying the success of Chinese society back in the 17th century, Gottfried Leibniz recognized the great value of learning from Confucianism.[2] Today, many timeless Confucian values remain inspiring. Herman Kahn predicted in 1979, "the Confucian ethic—the creation of dedicated, motivated, responsible, and educated individuals and the enhanced sense of commitment, organizational identity, and loyalty to various institutions—will result in all the neo-Confucian societies having at least potentially higher growth rates than other cultures."[3] Based on the early evidence of the Asian economic miracle and its linkage to Confucianism, Roderick MacFarquhar declared in 1980: "That ideology [Confucianism] is as important to the rise of the east Asian hyper-growth economies as the conjunction of Protestantism and the rise of capitalism in the West."[4]

The power of many Confucian values can be seen in widespread and compelling data and facts throughout history. Here we can point to the impact of Confucian values on ancient and modern China and other Confucianism-influenced countries as well as ethnic Chinese and Asians living in the US.

1. Ancient Chinese Civilization and Confucianism

If Greece and the Roman Empire represent Ancient Western Civilization, China represents a key cornerstone of Oriental Civilization. For much of ancient history, China was the most advanced and civilized country in the world. It led the world in technological and economic development until Europe advanced its technology and economy following the Industrial Revolution of the 18th century. The Chinese invented advanced iron/steel making, farming, porcelain, silk, transportation, paper, printing, shipping, and navigation technologies that enabled China to reach much higher levels of productivity and economic prosperity.[5] In 1600, China's GDP comprised 29% of the world's total while the whole of Western Europe comprised only 20%.[6] Chinese culture and social and political systems were admired and learned by many nations, both neighboring and distant. One interesting historical development was that, during the 13th and 17th centuries, China was conquered by Mongols and Manchus, respectively. However, after the conquerors entered China, they discovered the social and economic systems there were far more advanced than their own. As a result, they adapted themselves to the Chinese social-political systems in order to sustain their power. The conquerors were absorbed by the mighty Chinese culture, not the other way around as was typically the case.

What is it about Chinese civilization that makes it so long lasting and resilient? One key factor involves the cultural values upheld by Chinese society. What was the most distinguished Chinese cultural value? Confucianism. During the Han Dynasty, the Emperor Han Wudi in 133 BC officially adopted Confucian philosophy as the official value system and basis for China's political system. Confucius was regarded as the "Great Sage," and his moral value systems have impacted almost every Chinese family ever since. Dynasty after dynasty, whether China was ruled by the Chinese or foreign invaders, Confucius' status and his influence were seldom challenged, helping China to grow into a powerful nation over the next 2,000 years.

After China had become an economic, political, and cultural center of the Far East, its influence spread beyond the national boundaries. Many surrounding countries were eager to learn the Chinese economic and political systems and cultural values. The cultures of Japan, Korea, and Singapore are deeply influenced by China and by the Confucian values.

In modern society, as a framework for a political system, Confucian values have become obsolete due to the prevalence of the modern democratic system and the rule of law in the 19th and 20th centuries. But the Confucian moral values that impact family and individual behaviors have been rejuvenated in the last five decades and are creating a very positive impact on human society.

2. Economic Success in China and Other Confucianism-Influenced Regions

The positive impact of Confucianism has manifested in the economic success of China and other Asian countries in recent decades.

Two decades after World War II, Japan realized rapid economic growth in the 1960s and '70s, becoming the world's second largest economy in 1968. Between the 1960s and 1990s, the Four Asian Mini-Dragons—Korea, Taiwan, Hong Kong, and Singapore—achieved their own phenomenal economic growth and joined the ranks of the industrial nations. Even at their early stage of economic development, Herman Kahn (1979) and Roderick MacFarquhar (1980) recognized what they called the Confucian Ethic as the essential contributing factor to the rapid economic development of Japan, Korea, Taiwan, Hong Kong, and Singapore. In 1980, MacFarquhar also foresaw the rise of China: "If the 'four modernizations' policy succeeds in transforming China over the next several decades, an economic power-house will rise in east Asia, by which the standard [set by] the economic miracles of the South Koreas and Singapores would seem like solar flares against the sun."[7]

This is an accurate description of what happened in China over the following three decades. Ever since the former Chinese leader, Deng Xiaoping, adopted the "Open and Reform Policy" in 1978, China has achieved double-digit GDP growth, and in 2010 it surpassed Japan to become the world's second largest economy.[8] The following chart shows a comparison between the GDP growth rate of the US and that of China during the last three decades. As shown by the dotted lines, on average, the annual U.S. growth rate was 2.8% while China has reached 10% since 1980.[9] As mentioned earlier, the size of the Chinese economy has increased from 301.5 billion U.S. dollars in 1980 to 5,878 billion U.S. dollars in 2010, an increase of more than 15 times.[10]

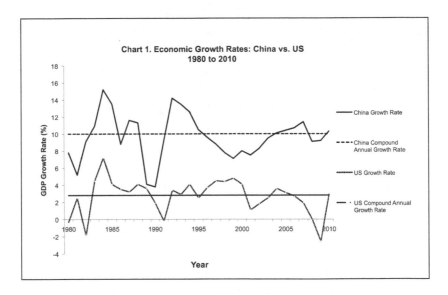

What are the key success factors of China's economic growth? Clearly it is not the communism doctrine because this has led to economic failure all over the world, as seen in the economic stagnancy of the Soviet Block and the demise of the Soviet Union. The economic reform (introducing a free market system and active industrial policies)

Deng Xiaoping initiated has contributed significantly to the rise of China. It is the Chinese cultural heritage, in particular the Confucian Ethic, that has created a huge impact from a human and cultural standpoint. In 1989, Tu Weiming, one of the world's leading scholars in Confucianism, Harvard professor in East Asian studies, and former director of the Harvard-Yenching Institute listed self-cultivation, hard work, family commitment, and an emphasis on education, along with other factors, as conducive to the rapid economic development of East Asia.[11] These qualities led to the creation of many highly motivated, hardworking, and well-educated workers, supportive families, and a progressive culture, which taken together contributed greatly to the economic success of China.

The successes of China, Japan, and the Asian Mini-Dragons are not limited to economic growth. They have expanded into many strategic areas: Japan is a world leader in consumer electronics and auto manufacturing. Korea and Taiwan have become world leaders in information technology. Korea is rapidly joining the ranks of those countries considered leaders in electronics, auto manufacturing, and other areas. Hong Kong and Singapore have become centers of regional finance and international trade. China has become the "world's factory" and has developed the nuclear bomb, long-range missiles, space technology, clean energy, and other high-tech industries. China is the third nation to successfully send astronauts into space on its own rockets after the USSR and the US.[12] It has even started building its own space station. All of these countries offer top-notch education in mathematics and sciences.

As briefly described in the Introduction, according to the *2009 OECD Programme for International Student Assessment (PISA),* the world-renowned student assessment report, Shanghai-China, Korea, Hong Kong, Singapore, and Japan all ranked significantly higher than the US in mathematics and science education for 15-year-old students. With the exception of reading for Taiwanese students, which was just 5 points behind the US (US: 500; Taiwan: 495), all Confucianism-influenced countries/regions were among the leaders in educational achievement.[13]

Table 1. The 2009 PISA Ranking of the US and Select Asian Countries/Regions

(Out of 65 OECD and Partner Countries and Economies)

	Shanghai-China	Hong Kong	Taiwan	Singapore	Korea	Japan	USA
Reading	1	4	23	5	2	8	15
Mathematics	1	3	5	2	4	9	31*
Science	1	3	14	4	6	5	23

*US Mathematics score is below the OECD average.

Tony Jackson, Vice President of Education at the Asia Society, said on *ABC News*, "The 2009 PISA data demonstrate the rise in the quality of education in Asia — among the top performers were Shanghai, Hong Kong, Singapore, Japan, and Korea… Any definition of a world-class education must include knowledge of Asia and the language and cultural skills to deal with Asia. It's a two-way street: America must now learn from—and with —Asia and the world."[14]

Today, China is the largest supplier of educated workers in the world,with more than 5 million college graduates each year, and more than 2 million from science, technology, engineering and mathematics (STEM) fields. With economic growth and educational improvement, China has also increased its capacity for scientific research. Today, China's R&D spending forms 12% of the world's total, second only to the US. Before 2003, 1 out of 20 scientific articles in the world were published by researchers in China. From 2004 to 2008, that ratio has doubled, to 1 out of 10.[15] More scientific research will lead to more innovations in the future.

3. Model Minority: The Success of Chinese Americans and Asian Americans

If we want to take stock of a culture, the best gauge, other than national standing, is to look at the people. If people who share a similar culture excel across national borders, it is a clear indicator that the shared culture has contributed to their success. The following examples portray the success stories of Chinese people in the US and Southeast Asia, as well as successful Japanese Americans and Korean Americans, all of whom are influenced by Confucianism.

As an immigration country, the United States consists of many ethnic groups who have come from all over the world. Some of them have done very well, in terms of achieving the "American Dream" and contributing to the progress of the country. Asian Americans belong to this remarkable group and were recognized as the "Model Minority" in 1968 by William Petersen, who based his observation on Asian Americans' success in the United States.[16] Today, Asian Americans are regarded as "the highest-income, best-educated and fastest-growing racial group in the US."[17] Among them, Chinese Americans compose the largest Asian American ethnic group, and their successes in many aspects serve as a good representation of the "Model Minority."

a) Economic Success

Compared to American and European roots, Asian Americans arrived on this continent relatively late. The first Chinese immigrants came to the US about 160 years ago. However, on average, Asian Americans with a Confucianism tradition—Chinese, Japanese, and Korean Americans—have median household incomes significantly higher than the U.S. average. According to the 2009 U.S. Census, Chinese Americans ($69,502) and Japanese Americans ($64,231) earned a higher median household income than Non-Hispanic Whites ($54,671) and the Total US Population ($50,221). This is quite an achievement in light of their relatively recent arrival to America.[18]

Ethnic Chinese in Southeast Asian countries represent another economic success story. In countries including Indonesia, Malaysia, Thailand, Singapore, and Vietnam, 70% of total private and corporate capital is held by ethnic Chinese, who represent only about 6% of the total population. They are successful businessmen in almost every corner of Southeast Asia.[19] In recent decades, Chinese businessmen have spread to Africa, Russia, and the Middle East, where they are duplicating a lot of their business success.

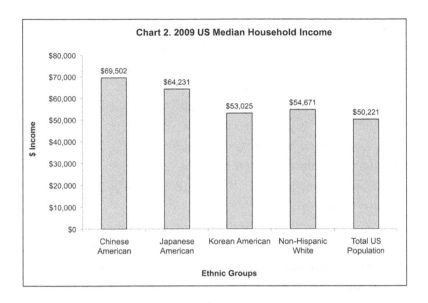

Chart 2. 2009 US Median Household Income

b) Education, Science, and Technology

Based on a 2012 Pew Research Center report, Chinese Americans (51.1%), Japanese Americans (46.1%), and Korean Americans (52.6%) all outperform the U.S. general population (28.0%) significantly in terms of their educational attainment, which is measured by holding a college undergraduate degree or higher.[20]

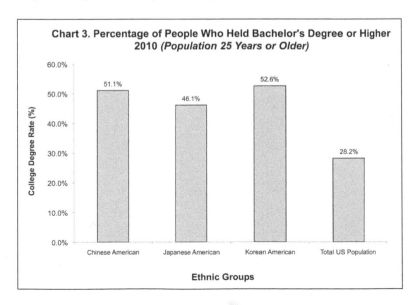

Chart 3. Percentage of People Who Held Bachelor's Degree or Higher 2010 (Population 25 Years or Older)

According to data from the National Center for Educational Statistics, Asian Americans score the highest on ACT and SAT tests.[21, 22] In 2009, their college enrollment rate was the highest in the country at 92.2% while the national average was only 70.1%.[23] Although Asian Americans form about 5.6% of the total U.S. population, they make up a significantly higher percentage of students in America's most prestigious universities: University of California at Berkeley (46%, 2007 data), Stanford University (24%, 2005 data), Massachusetts Institute of Technology (27%, 2005 data), Yale (14%, 2005 data), and Princeton (13%, 2005 data).[24]

In the science and technology arena, a higher percentage of Chinese Americans participate in the science and engineering fields, 18% vs. 5% of the national average.[25] They are closely tied to many scientific and engineering achievements. These include seven Nobel Laureates such as Daniel C. Tsui, Steven Chu, and Tsung-Dao Lee; *Time Magazine*'s 1996 Man of Year, AIDS research David Ho; world famous Architect I. M. Pei; and renowned forensic expert Henry Lee.[26] Today, many U.S. universities and other scientific and engineering institutions count Chinese Americans among their department chairs and leading professors and researchers. In many

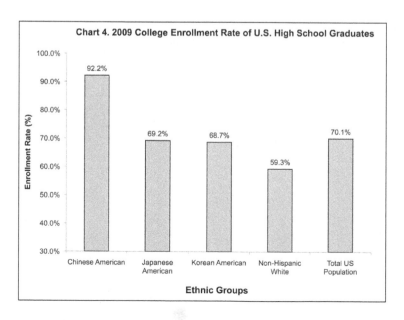

Chart 4. 2009 College Enrollment Rate of U.S. High School Graduates

high tech and engineering firms such as Intel, Microsoft, and Yahoo, Chinese Americans are among the top engineers who help keep the US on the cutting edge of the technology front. In the nation's most prestigious high school science competitions, including the *Intel Science Talent Search* and *Siemens Science Competition,* over the last five years, more than 20% of the national prizewinners have Chinese or East Asian heritage.[27,28]

It is worth mentioning that Chinese Americans have extended their achievements into many areas. In the political arena, Gary Locke, former governor of Washington State, Elaine Chao, former Secretary of Labor, and Steven Chu, Secretary of Energy of Obama Administration, are outstanding Asian American examples.[29]

c) Family Management and Crime Control

In addition to their economic and educational achievements, Asian Americans have also scored remarkably well in social behavior. Over the last decades, many statistics-based research reports have concluded that the crime rate of Asian Americans is the lowest among racial groups, about one quarter of the national average.[30] For example, in 2008, Asian Americans, who accounted for about 5.6% of the total

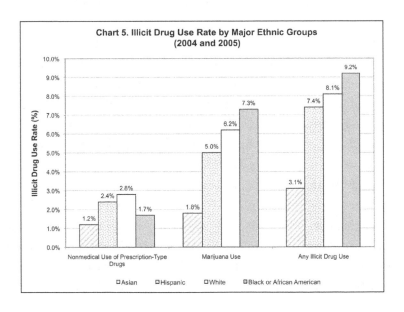

U.S. population, constituted only 1.1% of the total of those arrested for non-legal violent crimes and 1.3% of those arrested for property crimes.[31]

In a statistical breakdown of Illicit Drug Use Rate, among persons age 12 or older, by Major Ethnic Groups: 2004 and 2005, Asian Americans ranked the lowest at 3.1% while the other racial groups examined reach 7.4% and 9.2%.[32]

In a 2007 report issued by the US Department of Education, Asian American students collected all the gold medals for social behavior: lowest rates in use of alcohol, cigarettes, and illicit drugs; lowest rate of teenage pregnancy; lowest rates in the categories of "carried a weapon" and "engaged in a physical fight."[33]

Besides low crime rates and low illicit drug use, Asian Americans also demonstrate a high degree of family stability. Statistical data indicate the divorce rate (as measured by the number of divorces among a population 15 years or older) of Asian Americans and Chinese Americans is 4.2% and 3.8%, respectively, less than half the 9.7% national average.[34] The same pattern is found in the obesity prevention. In a 2004-2006 data that separate Asian and Chinese Americans as separate group, the obesity rates were only 8.1% for Asian American and 4.2% for Chinese American, while the national average was around 30%.[35]

If we take an overall view of what Asian Americans and Chinese Americans have achieved in economic, scientific, technological, and social arenas, it is quite an accomplishment for a minority group that has lived in the US for no more than 160 years. Being well educated, having a good income and stable family, encountering less trouble with crime, drug abuse, and other undesirable issues—Is that the American Dream many people strive to achieve?

Combined with the historical achievement of China, the rapid economic development of China, Japan, Korea, Taiwan, and Singapore, and the social/economic achievements of Chinese and Asian Americans, we can see all these things share a common cultural denominator: Confucian values. In the past, Confucianism contributed greatly to the ancient civilizations of the East. Today, it is still helping Chinese, Japanese, Koreans, and many others to succeed. *Long-lasting and inspiring, Confucian values are the secrets behind the success of Chinese/Asian Americans, as well as the economic miracles enacted by Japan, Korea, China, and other East Asian countries.*

Chapter 3.

Confucianism and Inspiring Confucian Values

3.1 Confucius and Confucianism

Confucius (孔夫子, Kong the Master) did not found a major religion, but his influence on human society is as great as that of Buddha, Jesus, or Mohamed. Confucius was one of the most important philosophers, thinkers, political advocators, and educators in Chinese history. The Confucianism he created, which was further developed by his disciples and followers, has influenced Chinese and other East Asian civilizations for more than 2,000 years.

Confucius, whose name was Kong Qiu (孔丘), was born in 551 BC in the northern Chinese state of Lu. Although Confucius' family came from noble origins in the state of Song, he lost his father at a young age and was raised by his mother under poor living conditions. Despite the hardships suffered, he devoted himself to learning. When Confucius was 17 years old, he was recognized as a very knowledgeable youth who had good respect for social norms. That year, Baron Li Meng, an official of Lu, asked his son to study under Confucius. Later on, Confucius was offered managerial positions in a warehouse, and later a dairy, where he built a reputation for effectiveness. A few years later, the Duke of Lu sponsored him to visit Zhou, the capital of the Zhou Dynasty (1046–221 BC, which Lu and other Chinese states belonged to) to learn *Li* (礼), the ritual and social norms. He met Taotz, the founder of Taoist philosophy, when he visited Zhou.

Between his 30s and 50s, Confucius grew into a distinguished thinker, educator, and political advocator. He established the first private school in Chinese history and educated 3,000 disciples. Many of them later became officials in various Chinese states and Confucian scholars, expanding Confucian influence widely. He visited many states in Northern China. He gave advice to various dukes of those states and promoted his social-political philosophies.

In his 50s, Confucius was offered an administrative position as a mayor in the state of Lu. He was quickly promoted to Minister of Justice and then Acting Premier within five years. Under his influence, Lu became better managed and stronger. He won back a large territory that had been captured by the neighboring state of Qi. However, Lu's success led to uneasiness in the state of Qi, which was jealous of Lu's accomplishment. In order to stop Lu's progress, the state of Qi selected 80 attractive young women. After dressing them up and training them to dance, the state of Qi presented them to the Duke and Baron of Lu. As predicted, the Duke of Lu soon became distracted by such entertainment and gradually abandoned his administrative tasks. This kind of self-indulgent behavior was a clear departure from Confucius' political philosophy, which suggested a king should rule a country by virtue and should establish model behavior for its ministers and citizens to follow. In protest, Confucius quit the job and left Lu.

Over the next 14 years, Confucius once again traveled widely, passing through many states. However, none of them officially adopted his political philosophy or offered him another major administrative position during this time. He came back to Lu in his late 60s and died in 478 BC at the age of 73.[1]

The time in which Confucius lived was a period in which the King of the Zhou Dynasty gradually declined in power and influence. China was being sliced into feudal states by warlord "dukes" who waged battles, pursued power and dominance, and taxed subjects heavily. The social order established by the Zhou Dynasty was collapsing. The nation cried out for solutions. What set Confucius apart from many youths at that time were his strong interests in history, society, and political systems, and his broad perspectives regarding nations and humanity. Despite having grown up in a poor family, Confucius did not focus his efforts on making a simple living. Instead, he devoted himself to formulating how to establish a reasonable political system, how to create a sound moral value system, how to restore the social order, and how to build an idealistic society. He absorbed the knowledge that existed at the time better than most people, and he thought much deeper than most people. As a result of his unparalleled thinking, he developed a moral value-based social-political system that would exert a far-reaching influence on China and the Far East for more than 2,000 years.

The social and political value systems established by Confucius and his followers are very comprehensive. They cover almost every aspect of governmental affairs, people's daily life, and the development of society. The main Confucian social-political values include:

1. Establish ren (仁)—"humanism," as the foundation of social and political affairs[2]

Treating people in a humane way, with a high moral regard (仁, pronounced as *ren*), is the fundamental value of Confucianism. Confucius defined *ren* as "loving people." Mencius (372–289 BC), the second most influential scholar of Confucianism, said, "A humane person loves other people. A person with good manners respects other people. A person who loves other people will always be loved. A person who respects other people will always be respected. (仁者爱人，有礼者敬人。爱人者，人恒爱之。敬人者，人恒敬之。)."[3] Confucius also specifically suggests that the standard for treating other people should be how you expect other people to treat you: "What you do not want done to yourself, do not do to others (己所不欲，勿施与人。)."[4] He encouraged the act of contributing to other people's happiness and discouraged the act of harming others. He stated, "A gentleman should do things to help others to achieve happy results, should not undermine others' happiness (君子成人之美，不成人之恶。)."[5]

2. Advocate ren-zheng (仁政)— governing by moral values[6]

Confucius envisioned a society governed by virtues. He was not satisfied with the political order achieved by vigorous administration and enforcement of criminal laws. He said, "Guiding people by government measures, and regulating them by the threat of punishment, the people will try to keep out of jail, but will have no sense of honor or shame. Guiding the people by virtue and regulating them by *li* (social norms, sense of propriety), the people will have a sense of right or wrong and have norms to follow (道之以政，齐之以刑，民免而无耻。道之以德，齐之以礼，有耻且格。)."[7]

Mencius further developed the concept of governing by moral values by asking the rulers to put the people's interests first. He said, "People have the highest priority, the next is the nation, and the third is the ruler (民为贵，社稷次之，君为轻。)."[8] It was the most humane conception of government at that time. Both Confucius and Mencius advocated that rulers treat citizens in a humane way. They were very critical of those dictators who ruled the country ruthlessly. As Confucius famously pointed out, "Tyranny is fiercer than a tiger (苛政猛于虎也)."[9]

3. Observe li (礼)—the rationalized social order[10]

As another essential part of his vision for a well functioning society, Confucius tried to restore a rationalized social order, one based on love for one's kind and respect for authority. This is reflected in one of the most famous Confucian behavior guidelines, "Ten Human Duties (十义)," which was first recorded in one of the Confucian classics, the

Book of Rites (礼记, pronounced as *li-ji*), later modified by Confucian scholars as:[11,12]

(1) *Fu-ci* (父慈): The father/parent should be devoted to and love their children.

(2) *Zi-xiao* (子孝): The children should respect and care for their parents.

(3) *Fu-he* (夫和): The husband should treat his wife well.

(4) *Qi-shun* (妻顺): The wife should support the husband's decisions.

(5) *Xiong-you* (兄友): The elder brother/sibling should treat the younger brother/sibling friendly.

(6) *Di-gong* (弟恭): The younger brother/sibling should treat the elder brother/sibling with respect.

(7) *Peng-xin* (朋信): Friends should treat each other with trust.

(8) *You-yi* (友义): Friends should help one another for the right cause.

(9) *Jun-jing* (君敬): The ruler should respect the ministers.

(10) *Chen-zhong* (臣忠): The ministers should be loyal to the ruler.

These social norms have two distinctive features: first, the love, or *ren*, between the people, such as "Parents should love their children;" second, the establishment of authority, such as "Ministers should be loyal to the ruler."

The *li* also include many principles and processes regarding human activities, such as education methods and procedures for major worship and festivals. Its aim is to establish a benign and orderly society.

It is worth mentioning that the norms advocated by Confucianism reflect a patriarchal social organization in which the rights of women and youths are not given equal weight, compared to today's modern standard. However, we need to keep in mind that Confucian social norms were formed 2,500 years ago when patriarchies were dominant across most major cultures, including Greek, Germanic, Roman, Hebrew, Arabian, and Indian. Compared to the barbarous dictatorships and slavery systems commonplace at the time, the social norms promoted by Confucianism represented one pinnacle of human civilization.

4. Endorse zhi (智)—knowledge and wisdom

Confucius believed in the power of knowledge. He provided his personal examples to illustrate the importance of learning. "At fifteen I determined to learn (吾十有五而志于学)."[13] He described himself as a persistent learner who "never loses interest in learning (学而不厌)."[14] In his view, while *ren* (humanism) was a basis for administrating the country, *zhi* (knowledge) was the basis for knowing the world and for distinguishing good from bad. Both Confucius and Mencius believed the administrators of the country should embody both *ren* (humanism) and *zhi* (knowledge). Like *ren, zhi* is one of the "Five Constant Virtues (五常)" that are considered essential moral guidelines by Confucian scholars.[15]

Recognizing the power of knowledge, Confucianism also emphasizes the importance of learning and education. Confucius pointed out that gentlemen comprehend principles through learning (君子学以致其道).[16] In the *Book of Rites,* Confucianism promotes respect for teachers and respect for learning: "If the teacher is respected, the knowledge is respected, and then people will value the learning (师严然后道尊，道尊然后民知敬学。)."[17] Confucius did not stop at preaching. He established the first recorded private school in China, and his disciples followed his traditions and established many schools after he passed away. It is worth mentioning that Confucius is among the first people in human history to initiate the concept of equal education opportunity. He advocated providing an education to everyone regardless of family background or social status (有教无类).[18]

5. Develop shi (士)—the intellectual upper class, to administrate the country[19]

In order to realize his political vision, Confucius stressed the need to develop qualified administrators for the country. He defined an intellectual upper class called *shi* (士) that must have both high moral values and knowledge to manage. In one of the *Four Confucian Classics, Great Learning* 《大学》, it says that in order to become a *shi*, a person should develop a sound moral value system and good personal behavior (修身), based on which he should be able to manage his family well (齐家), then administrate national affairs (治国) and bring peace to the world (平天下).[20]

Such prescriptions for national well-being are as well intentioned as they are specific. The social-political value systems Confucius developed are truly remarkable and among the most advanced for their time, which was 2,500 years ago, about 80 years before Socrates. At a time when most nations still adopted brutal slavery systems, he promoted humanism (*ren*) as a way to treat people humanely. When most of the world was still ruled by tyrants, he asked that a ruler govern his country by virtue. He endorsed the power of knowledge and promoted education. He also created the first meritocracy-based system in human history: Anybody could become a government official based on moral value and knowledge, rather than family origin or social status. With so many advanced ideas embedded in his teaching, Confucius was poised to generate a monumental impact on human history when he passed away in 478 BC.

Although no ruler adopted his social-political value system during his lifetime, Confucius had started to fundamentally change Chinese society through the philosophy and books he left behind, and more importantly, the teaching he conducted. His disciples had spread throughout China, becoming important officials or political advisors in various states in which they continued promoting the Confucian value systems. As many of his disciples became scholars, opening Confucian schools, his philosophy and social-political systems were further spread across China.

For 300 years following Confucius' death, China entered into a Warring States period (战国, 475–221BC), during which dukes of various nations fought one another to either expand or defend their territories. During the same time, more and more social-political value systems were formed. In addition to Taoism (called *Dao-jia* 道家) and Confucianism (called *Ru-jia* 儒家), which were formed earlier,

Mohism (called *Mo-jia* 墨家), Legalism (called *Fa-jia* 法家), and many other movements took shape. Suntzu, the great military strategist and author of *The Art of War,* also lived during this period. Scholars of many of these schools were promoting their ideas to various dukes for adoption. Historians refer to this period of Chinese history as a time of "100 schools of thought competing for a voice (百家争鸣)," which is reminiscent of Ancient Greece, when many philosophical ideas blossomed.

In 356 BC, the duke of the state of Qin (秦) initiated political reform by adopting Legalism, which emphasized the strict rule of law. In the century that followed, the economic and military power of Qin was strengthened as a result. In 221 BC, Qin Shihuang, the first emperor of China, conquered all other states and unified the country. He established the Qin Dynasty (秦朝, 221–207BC). However, because of his brutal rule, the Qin Dynasty lasted only 15 years. During his rule, he burned most books he could find and buried about 400 scholars alive, many of whom were Confucians.

After overthrowing the Qin Dynasty and having learned a lesson from Qin-Shi-Huang's brutal rule, the emperor of the Han Dynasty (汉朝, 202BC–9AD) started to search for alternative social-political philosophies. Around 133 BC, Emperor Han Wudi officially adopted Confucianism as the national value system, an act that would mark one of the most important milestones in both the history of Confucianism and the history of China.[21]

For centuries afterwards, Confucius was regarded as the "Great Sage" (文圣, for all social sciences). Temples to Confucius were built in his hometown and throughout the country. Schools teaching Confucianism were opened in almost every city in China. Many emperors, in a show of respect to Confucius or to emphasize Confucianism, have given Confucius various honorary titles. As mentioned earlier, the two major conquerors of China, the Mongols who established the Yuan Dynasty (元朝, 1206–1368) and the Manchus who established the Qing Dynasty (清朝, 1616–1911), both gave Confucius honorary titles and nominated a great many Confucians for various minister positions.

Since its adoption in 133 BC, Confucianism has been the dominant social-political value system in China, until 1911, when the Republic of China was established.

The adoption of Confucianism contributed directly to China's ascent to a politically stable and economically prosperous civilization, unmatched by any other nation for 2,000 years. Influenced by the Confucian value of governing by virtue, Chinese emperors took responsibility to build infrastructure, manage nationwide disaster relief, and take up many other social responsibilities. Many of them reduced taxation to a sustainable level that encouraged farming and economic development. As early as 2,000 years ago, during the Han Dynasty, the Chinese government undertook a policy of regulating the agriculture market. The government bought up grain when there was a surplus and sold it when there was a shortage. It was a wise measure that shielded the significant risk of farming, which depends heavily on Mother Nature. It stabilized the grain price for both farmers and consumers. Today, the Chinese government continues this tradition.

The Confucian endorsement of knowledge and promotion of education contributed greatly to many technological innovations in ancient China. As we introduced earlier, technology advancement in iron/steel making, farming, paper, printing, and navigation helped make China the most prosperous economy in the world. This held true until the Industrial Revolution got underway in England in the 18th century and thereafter accelerated the growth of Western economies.

The social norms, laws, and regulations established in China were also very advanced for the time. "Indeed it is difficult," wrote Gottfried Leibniz in 1699, "to describe how beautifully all the laws of the Chinese, in contrast to those of other peoples, are directed to the achievement of public tranquility and the establishment of social order."[22]

As a result, China became the economic, political, and cultural center of the East. Many nations sent ambassadors and students to China to learn Chinese culture, technology, and political systems. Gradually, many aspects of Chinese culture, including Confucianism, were adopted by surrounding nations, including Korea and Japan.

Today, the beautifully written Chinese poems of the Tang Dynasty (唐朝, 618–907) are still included in Japanese elementary school textbooks. Each year, Koreans still hold a grand ceremony to commemorate Confucius on his birthday. Confucian influence also can be seen in Singapore, where many ethnic Chinese reside.

3.2 THE INFLUENCE OF CONFUCIAN VALUES ON CHINESE SOCIETY

After the adoption of Confucianism as the national social and political value system, two events significantly enhanced the spread of Confucianism into Chinese secular society.

1. The official establishment of the Imperial Examination System[23]

Under the influence of Confucianism, since the Han Dynasty, many governmental officials had been selected based on moral and knowledge credentials. Initially, the candidates were recommended by government officials at various levels. However, this approach did not apply a unified standard to every candidate. About 700 years later, the first emperor of the Sui (隋朝, 581–618) Dynasty, Sui Wendi, formally established the Imperial Examination System (Called *ke-ju-zhi-du*, 科举制度), which used national exams to select and recruit bureaucrats. The system typically was organized at local, provincial, and national levels. The candidates who passed the local tests would have a chance to take the provincial tests. If they passed these, they were given a chance to participate in the national tests. Those who excelled in the national and provincial tests were appointed to various government posts. Influenced by Confucianism, the Imperial Examination System adopted the principle of "equal opportunity." It was open to everyone regardless of family background or social status. After its establishment, every Chinese (male at that time) had a chance to become a government official as long as he studied hard and passed the national exam. This institutionalized Confucius' revolutionary idea of replacing nobility of blood with nobility of virtue (and knowledge), a hallmark of meritocracy.

The impact created by the establishment of the Imperial Examination System on Chinese society was twofold. First, it led to the rapid spread of Confucianism. As Confucianism was inherent in the Imperial Examination, people started to learn more about it, through its books and its teachings, in order to pass the Imperial Examination. Second, it created a direct career path linking education with career advancement and family happiness. Similar to many other nations at that time, ancient China was a hierarchic society. The emperor held the highest position, next came the ministers, then various governmental officials, and finally other professions. A person's status was directly related to their wealth, social respect, and degree of happiness. The establishment of the Imperial Examination System created an upward mobility avenue, a social ladder open to everyone. The "Ancient Chinese Dream" then became to pass the Imperial Examination and become a government official. Many people joined in the competition, in the hopes of attaining a prestigious social status.

More than 2,000 years of ancient Chinese history has produced many touching stories about the pursuit of this "Ancient Chinese Dream." Many poor but ambitious youths had to overcome financial difficulties and study hard to pass the local exams. After clearing the first hurdle they had to raise funds from relatives and travel hundreds or even thousands miles, many times on foot, to attend the provincial and national exams. Some were lucky, successfully passing the national exam to bring honor, wealth, and status to their families. Many others were unable to get that far, however, because of the competitive nature of the exams.

In Western culture, there is the story of Cinderella, in which a beautiful but poor girl overcomes an abusive stepmother and finds happiness by marrying the prince. In ancient China, the story of Cinderella was portrayed very differently. Many ancient Chinese dramas told the following romantic tale: A poor, but talented young man falls in love with a beautiful and well-mannered girl from a rich family. The girl is deeply impressed by his talents, in particular his beautiful poetry. They love each other wholeheartedly. However, because of his poverty, the girl's parents forbid their marriage. But the young man did not give up. He studied hard and placed first (called *zhuang-yuan*, 状元 in Chinese) in the national Imperial Exam. Once he had earned the honor and appointment of an important government post, the girl's parents changed their attitude. The young man finally was able to marry his beloved.

This story illustrates how ancient China already had established a culture that emphasized education, stressed hard work, and encouraged upward mobility for anyone who had a dream.

2. Popularization of Confucianism starting from the Song Dynasty

During the Song Dynasty (960–1279 AD), Confucianism reached another peak. A renowned scholar named Zhu Xi (朱熹，1130–1200) spent his whole life studying Confucianism and selected four books to stand as the classics of Confucianism: *Analects,* 《论语》, *Mencius,* 《孟子》, *Great Learning* 《大学》, and *Central Harmony* 《中庸》.[24] These four volumes thereafter were referred to as the *Four Books* in Chinese history. Zhu Xi also "interpreted" the *Four Books,* in effect translating them from complex ancient Chinese into plain language that could be better understood by laymen. Since then the *Four Books* have been designated as the official textbooks for schools, and their contents were often tested in China's Imperial Exams.

Another scholar of the Song Dynasty, Wang Yingling (王应麟, 1223–1296), authored an educational poem titled "Three Word Chant" 《三字经》.[25] It is approximately 1,000 words long and organized into three words per phrase. In addition to providing basic knowledge for children and a concise summary of Chinese history, "Three Word Chant" embodies many Confucian values and lists key moral principles of Confucianism. It also stresses the need to set up career objectives at an early age, to study hard, and to become a good contributor to the family and the country.

The creation of "Three Word Chant" was revolutionary because for the first time it made Confucianism widely accessible. It soon was adopted as required reading for elementary school students in

China. In the centuries following its introduction, almost every school child in China was asked to memorize "Three Word Chant." Confucianism, therefore, was spread to nearly every family in China through the *Four Books* and "Three Word Chant." In ancient China, the popularity of these two works mirrored that of the *Bible* in the Christian nations today.

3.3 THE EVOLUTION OF SECULAR CONFUCIAN VALUES

After Confucianism became the dominant social-political value system in China, the Chinese people directly applied many relevant ethical and social values of Confucianism to guide various aspects of their daily lives such as work ethic, money management, family affairs, and friendship. These same secular Confucian values have since been used by Chinese families generation after generation. For example, in the money management area, the Confucian values of saving and thrift (节俭) are widely adopted by most Chinese families. In terms of work ethic, hard work and high motivation (勤奋) have become the norms of Chinese workers.

In some areas, however, the original Confucian values were based on restrictive moral standards. For example, in ancient times, most Chinese students were taught to become morally sound government officials. They were advocated to control all selfish motives and pursue a higher mission to serve the country. A person was required to wake up early, study and work hard, and sit straight. He was expected to act politely when meeting seniors, his teachers, or upper level officials. He was required to control his desires and emotions. With this kind of orthodox Confucianism, personal objectives, or family interests, if any, were given a much lower priority than grand missions of "administrating national affairs and bringing peace to the world." Original Confucianism did not emphasize gaining wealth or fame for families or individuals.

Nevertheless, Chinese culture is very pragmatic. Over the centuries, Chinese people have creatively adapted many Confucian values to suit their needs in building a successful career and pursuing family happiness. In "Three Word Chant", personal/family objectives are no longer taboo, but something everybody can pursue. The focus of setting up an ambitious career goal, *li-zhi* (立志), has been modified to include realizing personal achievement to bring wealth and honor to one's family, in addition to the original goal of serving the country. It gives many examples describing how a person achieved career objectives that not only contributed to society, but also brought honor and wealth to their families. In practice, many Chinese realized the benefit of setting up ambitious career objectives. In application, it is closely related to their individual and/or family goals.

Another example is education. Confucius emphasized education as a way to improve one's moral standards and to increase knowledge. After the Imperial Examination System was established in China, education became a common means by which regular citizens climbed the social ladder in pursuit of a better life. Again, "Three Word Chant" gives many good examples of people who studied hard and achieved their career objectives. Although not all students were able to attain a governmental position, the knowledge gained during the education process generated positive benefits in their life. As a result, education has become a mandate for every Chinese family that can afford it.

If we say that the pragmatism of the Chinese people has transformed many Confucian values from doctrines that relate only to social elites or scholars of society to a set of secular values that can pertain to everybody's daily life, it is the introduction of—or very often clash with—modern Western values that results in the extinction of outdated Confucian values.

Like most social-political value systems established by other great thinkers, Confucianism carries with it characteristics of the founder's time and its shortcomings. As I pointed out earlier, Confucian influence took root 2,500 years ago when patriarchy and loyalty to the king were the dominant social norms across almost all major cultures. Due to the cultural limitations of Confucius and other Confucian scholars, some traditional Confucian values are not appropriate in light of today's standards. For example, women were not recognized as having equal rights. Children were rarely allowed to challenge or argue with their parents. In some cases, its implementation went to extremes. Widows were forbidden to get remarried. If the emperor requested that a minister give his life, the minister was expected to comply regardless of the soundness of the emperor's decision.

However, these kinds of Confucian values have been totally overturned during the last few centuries as Western influences spread into oriental countries. Since the mid nineteenth century, after its successful industrial revolution, Western influence gradually penetrated into China. In 1911, Dr. Sun Yat-Sen established the Republic of China, putting an end to more than 3,000 years of political systems ruled by various dynasties. Dr. Sun tried, though unsuccessfully, to introduce the democratic system into China. In 1949, Mao Zedong established the People's Republic of China, officially introducing Communism into the state. Thirty years later, in 1978, Chinese leader Deng Xiaoping launched the Open and Reform Policy, which introduced advanced Western economic management methods and technologies into China.

These dramatic social-political changes have also reshaped the social and ethical value systems in China. Chinese people have abolished the "Three Cardinal Guides of Confucianism (三纲)," which defines the interrelationships among the emperor-minster, father-son, and husband-wife, with the emperor, father, and husband playing leading roles.[26] Today, women in China can go to school and work and hold political positions, and have the freedom to choose their spouse, divorce, and get remarried. Kids can argue with their parents while still holding high respect for them. In the 21st century, no government official is willing to die on behalf of a communist party leader. The social and political changes of the last few centuries have introduced a lot of modern value systems into Chinese culture and removed some outdated Confucian values from Chinese society.

Given historical evolution and the Western influence of the last few centuries, what were left are modern, secular Confucian values that are progressive and resilient.

1. *Li-zhi* (立志): Determination for an outstanding life.
2. *Zhi* (智): Respect for knowledge and knowledgeable people.

3. *Qin-xue* (勤学): Pursuing an excellent education, the sure road toward a happy life.
4. *Qin-fen* (勤奋): Working hard and being highly motivated.
5. *Jie-jian* (节俭): Thrift; saving for a better life.
6. *Gu-jia* (顾家): Caring for your family, in particular devotion to the next generation.
7. *Ren* (仁): Treating people humanely. Emphasizing interpersonal relationships.
8. *Xin* (信): Trust; living up to one's word.
9. *Yi* (义): Justice; willingness to make an effort/sacrifice for your friends for the right cause.
10. *Ze-you* (择友): Developing desirable friendships.
11. *Li* (礼):Observing social norms; being respectful.
12. *Zun-lao-ai-you* (尊老爱幼): Respecting seniors and caring for the young.

These are the lasting secular Confucian values that have evolved over the course of many dynasties and political systems. They have been deeply rooted in the psyche of most Chinese people, passed from one generation to the next. Amazingly, many modern Chinese, without even having to read Confucian books directly, unknowingly follow many Confucian principles in dealing with their education, work, and life. This is because many Confucian values have become embedded in Chinese society and the family culture of many Chinese people.

What is their impact on modern Chinese society? On the one hand, they create a highly motivated, competitive society: Most parents set high expectations for their children and spend a lot of time, effort, and expense on their education. Most students study very hard in order to be accepted to the top-ranked universities. Most employees work very hard in order to earn a promotion or a raise. Most people manage their money wisely, always saving for a rainy day. These phenomena, which are common in those societies influenced by Confucianism, illustrate the progressive and competitive side of secular Confucian values.

On the other hand, in order to establish appropriate moral standards and reduce the tension created by this high degree of competition, Confucianism advocates that people treat one another nicely, be trustful, respectable, and tolerant, and provide help to friends and care for the young and the elderly. This illustrates the bonding and harmonious side of secular Confucian values.

As a balanced combination of competitive and harmonious principles, secular Confucian values have become a grand cultural locomotive, driving China and East Asian countries in their rapid economic development and guiding Chinese and many Asian Americans to succeed in the US.

3.4 SELECTION OF FIVE INSPIRING CONFUCIAN VALUES

Out of the 12 modern secular Confucian values we listed, I believe the following five values are essential to help many Americans to improve their lives:

1. *Li-zhi* (立志): **Determination for an outstanding life.**
2. *Qin-xue* (勤学): **Pursuing an excellent education.**
3. *Jie-jian* (节俭): **Thrift; saving for a better life.**
4. *Gu-jia* (顾家): **Caring for your family.**
5. *Ze-you* (择友): **Developing desirable friendships.**

When I made this selection, my criteria focused on those areas that were lacking or had fallen behind in American society. I did not select values that I believe are already prevalent in American society. Based on my personal experience living in both China and the US, I believe that many of the moral values promoted by Christianity in the US are very similar to those promoted by Confucianism, such as trust, justice, integrity, treating people humanely, and caring for the young and the elderly. In many areas, Western societies are doing significantly better than China and other developing nations, such as in trust and integrity. In the US, in most cases, people do not have to worry about fake or unsafe products. But in China, such products are still a big concern for consumers. Moreover, the American approach of treating people equally is clearly better than the current Chinese practice of treating people according to status and seniority. As a result, although

I support the principles of *ren* (仁)—humanism, *yi* (义)—justice; *xin* (信)—trust, *li* (礼)—being respectful, and *zun-lao-ai-you* (尊老爱幼)—respecting the elderly and caring for the young, they are not the focus of this book.

Although it is one of the key success factors of Chinese society, I did not select the value of working hard and being highly motivated (勤奋) because we believe that Americans have one of the best work ethics and there is little need for me to emphasize this area. I have also incorporated the concept of *zhi* (智)—respect for knowledge and knowledgeable people into my discussion of *qin-xue* (勤学)—pursuing an excellent education.

The five values I selected primarily reflect the progressive side of secular Confucian values. After reading the next five chapters you will see how these five Confucian values address the most essential aspects of a person's life. *Li-zhi* sets up a bright and positive aspiration for your career and life. *Qin-xue* equips you with skills to aid in your career development as well as your ability to make good life decisions. *Jie-jian* teaches you to manage your money conservatively and wisely. *Gu-jia* guides you to create a stable and happy family and, especially, raise successful children. And *ze-you* helps you avoid bad influences and develop relationships beneficial to your life and career development. These values guide people toward successful lives and happy families. It is these inspiring values that contributed greatly to the recovery of the Japanese economy after World War II, the economic miracle of the Four Asian Mini-Dragons—Korea, Taiwan, Hong Kong, and Singapore—and in particular, the rise of China since the 1980s. These same values helped overseas Chinese succeed in Southeast Asian, moving up the social ladders in the US to become a "Model Minority" in American society. ***They are the untold Chinese and Asian secrets for success!***

PART II.

The Five Inspiring Confucian Values

AFTER READING MY SELECTION of five secular Confucian values, some readers may think: *Most of these values already exist in Western cultures. I already know such principles. I know that I need set up a career objective; I know I need to study hard; I know I need to care for my family; and I know how to choose friends.*

It is true that most Americans appreciate these principles. However, the difference is the level of the objectives you set for you or your children, the approaches you use to handle getting an education, the tradeoff you make when dealing with family, money, and friend issues, and more importantly, the determination you have and the extra effort you are willing to make to attain these things. It is these practices in Chinese American families that set them apart, enable them to do better

47

than average Americans in getting a high-quality education, having a good job, and making a prosperous living, as illustrated in Chapter 2.

In Part II, Chapters 4 to 8, I will talk about each selected Confucian value in great detail: What is the importance of each Confucian value? What are the Confucian principles and guidelines behind each value? And very importantly, how do Chinese Americans apply Confucian values to their daily lives to make them successful?

Here, I'd like to point out that such practices are not limited to Chinese or Chinese American families. There are many successful individuals/families from other ethnic groups who also emphasize education, saving, and active family management. I use successful Chinese Americans as examples simply because they directly benefit from the Confucian cultural heritage and their practice reflects distinctive cultural features. I call them "Confucianism-influenced Chinese American families" in this book.

As I wrote in the introduction, this is the "best practice sharing" approach I use throughout the book. My purpose in illustrating the good practices of Chinese Americans in implementing Confucian values is to help readers to better understand and utilize inspiring Confucian values. It is not to paint Chinese Americans as a perfect ethnic group with no faults, nor to portray every Chinese American family as an ideal, model family. Like other ethnic groups, Chinese Americans have their weaknesses, challenges, and unsuccessful families. They also can learn and benefit from the strengths of other cultures. It is the good Confucian practices from their cultural heritage, in combination with the strengths of Western culture, that help them to become a "Model Minority." And it is these good practices that people can benefit from!

Chapter 4.

First Value: *Li-zhi* (立志)

"Determination for an Outstanding Life"—
Confucian Value for Defining a Grand Destiny

What is *li-zhi* (立志)? *Li-zhi* is setting up an ambitious goal for your career and for your life. Translated formally, it means "to have a career/ life aspiration." Translated informally, it means "to have a big dream" for your life.

"Having a big dream" is essential for a person's future achievement. According to motivation theory, people make efforts based on identification of a need, a goal you want to pursue. If you set up a goal both ambitious and achievable, it is likely that you will have the willingness to exert a high level of effort toward attaining that goal. This means that you are motivated. On the other hand, if you set up an easy goal, you can achieve that with very little effort. There is little motivation for you to work harder and little chance to reach a higher level of achievement.

4.1 THE IMPORTANCE OF *LI-ZHI* IN MODERN AMERICAN LIFE

The US is a country exemplified by its achievements and people's pursuit of the American Dream. In the last two centuries, the US has produced many great achievers such as Thomas Edison, Andrew Carnegie, Henry Ford, Bill Gates and Steve Jobs. Their efforts have helped the US become the world's most economically, politically, and militarily powerful country in the 20th century.

In the 21st century, while most Americans are highly motivated to pursue their American Dreams, there are increasing numbers among the younger generations that either lack motivation or are motivated by unrealistic goals.

Today, too many American children are not motivated to perform adequately in their most crucial task: learning. Even with one of the most highly funded education systems in the world, the US lags behind many industrial and Asian countries. Among the key reasons behind such poor educational performance: a lack of student motivation and ambitious goals for academic achievement. In 1990, the Office of Educational Research and Improvement, U.S. Department of Education held a national conference on student motivation and identified a number of issues associated with low student motivation in the US.[1] In a 2003 study of teacher shortage, it was found that poor student motivation contributed to 17% of teacher turnover.[2] In 2006, Patrick Welsh, an English teacher at T. C. Williams High School in Alexandria, Virginia wrote a column in *USA Today* in which he pointed out an unpleasant truth about learning in the US. Many American kids lack the willingness and motivation to learn. They do not make the same level of effort as the young children of recent immigrants.[3] On September 6, 2010, Robert Samuelson wrote in a column printed in the *Washington Post*:

> *The larger cause of [the U.S. educational] failure is almost unmentionable: shrunken student motivation.... Motivation is weak because more students (of all races and economic classes, let it be added) don't like school, don't work hard and don't do well. In a 2008 survey of public high school teachers, 21 percent judged student absenteeism a serious problem; 29 percentage cited "student apathy."*[4]

A lack of motivation and effort leads to poor performance. As pointed out in Chapter 1, according to the 2009 OECD Global Education Assessment Report, U.S. 15-year-olds are seriously behind in mathematics (25th out of 34 OECD countries), scoring just about average in science (17th out of 34), and a little bit above average in reading (14th out of 34). Separately, according to data from national educational assessments, only one fifth of today's 8th graders in the US are proficient or advanced in math.[5] According to an *NPR News* report of July 24, 2011, every year one million students (~25%) drop out of high school.[6] That clearly represents a disappointing performance for the US, the world's most advanced nation.

If we look at colleges, the situation is even more alarming. Many colleges have earned reputations as "party schools" where students value having a good time more than studying. Many American college students pay more attention to sports and movie stars than facts impacting their lives, such as the economy, history and policies. A lack of motivation to learn also leads to poor results. The 53% college graduation rate (within six years) in the US is a huge educational failure. As a comparison, in many less developed countries, many high school students strive to compete for very limited college enrollment opportunities. If admitted, most of them will study very hard and receive the college degree on time because they appreciate the precious opportunity to enter college and the high cost of tuition they or their parents have to pay.

What does low motivation in education mean? It means more and more poorly educated youths will enter the workforce. They typically will create less wealth than educated people and in turn they will live a poorer life. According to a study by Georgetown University based on 2007-2009 statistics, in his or her lifetime, a high school dropout will earn $330,000 less than a high school graduate, almost $1.3 million less than a college graduate, and almost $1.7 million less than a Master's degree holder.[7] As discussed in Chapter 1, the more the national educational level is reduced, the less national wealth will be created and the more the national living standard will drop. On the one hand, a lack of motivation to learn has become a serious challenge facing the US.

On the other hand, misguided by sports/celebrity-centric pop culture, many American children are motivated by unrealistic goals. In the US, pop culture and mass media coverage have created a host of misleading influences on the citizens and in particular on children. It is widely reported the huge annual income sports stars such as Mike Jordon or Tiger Woods make during their sport careers. As a result, sports stars have attracted a tremendous amount of attention in American society. They are often regarded as role models for the young although most youths cannot remotely relate to the living conditions and extravagant lifestyles of such people.

The media likewise is obsessed with movie, TV, and music stars, creating widespread influence in today's American society. They focus on the entertainment aspect of their stories: their show performances, circulating gossip, and lifestyles. Thus it results in the misguided message that life is about having fun and there is no need to study, work hard, or lead a disciplined life. Reality shows such as "American Idol," "America's Got Talent," and "Who Wants to Be a Millionaire?" give the unrealistic impression that anyone can become rich and famous overnight, like winning the lottery. Unfortunately, pop culture has helped to create a "national epidemic of get-rich-quickism and something-for-nothingism," as Thomas Friedman wrote in his column of September 11, 2010.[8]

This kind of unbalanced media attention clearly dwarfs that given to those who want to pursue a good education, to become an engineer, architect, lawyer, accountant, or other education-based professional. It creates the illusion—in fact an implicit media orientation—that being a celebrity is an easy path to success. The reality, however, is just the opposite. To make it as a sports star, in addition to the incredibly hard work involved, a person has to be blessed with an array of natural talent and skill—things like body strength, flexibility, speed, response, and coordination. Without the talent, no matter how much practice is involved, a person will never become a successful professional sports star. For the same reason, not everyone has a realistic chance to become a successful singer. Although movie or TV stars do not require the same kind of talent as a sports star, the possibility to become a movie or TV star is vastly smaller than it is to become a successful engineer, doctor, lawyer, or businessman.

To be fair, many people are very talented in sports, the arts, singing, and acting. For them, to be motivated to pursue such careers is the right thing to do. For most children, however, being motivated to pursue more mainstream careers (such as engineer, manager, accountant, lawyer, doctor, and teacher) is the viable way toward economically secure lives.

Among those students who want to pursue mainstream careers, there is a significant mismatch among students' interests, their capability, and the job market of today and for the foreseeable future. As discussed in Chapter 1, with technology advancement, more and more jobs are created in the science, technology, engineering, and math (STEM) areas. According a report published by *Fortune* on May 20, 2011, "only 16% of American students in their senior year of high school have both math proficiency and an interest in pursuing a career in the STEM disciplines.... What we know is that few 12th graders are interested in these disciplines, about 50% switch to other majors in college, only 19% graduate with a STEM degree and only 10% of those go into STEM jobs."[9]

When the younger generations are not motivated to learn, or are motivated by unrealistic or impractical objectives, it creates a double-edged sword. On the one hand, it leads to a serious talent shortage in the U.S. labor market—with skilled engineers in particular. As a result, American corporations have to resort to importing skilled workers from other countries to fill the desperately needed engineering positions. In 2008 alone, more than 276,000 H1B visas were granted to foreign-born workers with college degrees or higher, with at least 200,000 going to engineering and science-related jobs, the majority of those in computer engineering.[10] The shortage forecast for the future is even more dire. According to a study by Georgetown University, "the US will be short as many as 3 million high-skill workers by 2018 [in the STEM areas]."[11]

On the other hand, many American students are not qualified to land well paid engineering jobs. Many of them end up with lower paid service type jobs. As a result, many among the younger generations are experiencing a decline in their quality of life.

4.2 THE CONFUCIAN VALUE OF *LI-ZHI* (立志): DETERMINATION FOR AN OUTSTANDING LIFE

In Confucianism, *li-zhi* is a key step for many youths in establishing their career objectives, and developing their moral value system and administrative capabilities, in order to become a valuable asset for the country. In the centuries after Confucius, many Confucian scholars further refined this core Confucian value about life into many inspiring guidelines:

1. Determination to have an outstanding career

Confucianism highly values those who are able to make a big difference during their lifetime. Confucius said, "A gentleman is ashamed to die without having accomplished something (君子疾 没世而名不称焉)."[12] As we mentioned earlier, in the Confucian classic *Great Learning*, Confucianism advocates one should develop a sound moral value system and personal capability (修身), based on which he should manage his family well (齐家), then administrate national affairs (治国) and bring peace to the world (平天下).[13] This is the aspiration that Confucianism inspires in every Chinese who wants to make a difference for their country. In his day Confucius looked down on the man who would "feed himself every day living without a purpose (饱食终日，无所用心)."[14] In Confucianism's view, life is too precious to be lived as mediocre.

Zhu Guo Liang (诸葛亮, 181–234 AD), a renowned prime minister and general in the Three Kingdom Period, further promoted this concept in his famous essay, "Advice to My Nephew 《诫外甥书》": "One shall set up his career goal to reach high and far (志当存高远)."[15] The determination to be outstanding has come to characterize the Confucian view of life.

2. Set up goals for different life stages

Confucianism does not stop at setting up an ambitious goal. It advocates setting up key milestones at key life stages. Confucius said, "At fifteen I determined to learn. At thirty I had established myself. At forty I had no more perplexities. After fifty I knew the will of heaven. At sixty nothing that I heard disturbed me. At seventy I could let my thought wander without trespassing the moral law (吾十有五而志于学，三十而立，四十而不惑，五十而知天命，六十而耳顺，七十而从心所欲，不逾矩。)."[16] What Confucius described about his life experience has become a benchmark for many Chinese to follow. Among them the most important is the key milestone at thirty years old: Establish yourself. In Chinese society, year thirty is when a person should have completed his or her study, become established in a career, and started a family.

In "Three Word Chant," the secular bible of Confucianism, it calls for all young students to set a career aspiration when they are young (尔小生，宜立志).[17] As a result, having a career goal when you are young and establishing yourself by the age of thirty has become a general standard for Chinese people to live by.

3. Be willing to make an extraordinary effort and sacrifice in order to achieve your ambitious goal

It takes extraordinary effort to achieve an extraordinary goal. Mencius outlined this principle more than 2,300 years ago. He envisioned a true gentleman as a person whom God will assign great responsibility. However, God would challenge him with both spiritual and physical suffering through which he can strengthen the willpower and endurance necessary for him to achieve his destiny (天将降大任于斯人也，必先苦其心志，劳其筋骨，饿其体肤，空乏其身，行弗乱其所为，所以动心忍性，曾益其所不能。).[18] Zhu Guo Liang (诸葛亮), in his famous essay "Advice to My Son《诫子书》", pointed out a similar principle in a very concise way: One should make a sacrifice—control today's desires in order to achieve his career aspiration (淡泊明志).[19]

4. Be resilient, never give up on your big dream

In order to achieve an outstanding goal, one may encounter extraordinary difficulties. This requires extraordinary resilience. That is what Confucianism promotes. In one of the Confucian classics, *Book of Changes* (易经), it says, "Heaven operates with a strong force; a gentleman shall be strong and never give up (天行健，君子以自强不息)."[20] Confucius also said: "You can kill the general in an army, but you cannot kill the ambition in a common man (三军可夺帅也，匹夫不可夺志也)."[21]

From this you can see the Confucian value on motivation includes many essential elements in building a person's character: setting up ambitious objectives, working hard, exercising strong willpower, being resilient, having the ability to persevere. All of them are essential for a person's success, both in their career and in their life.

As discussed in Chapter 3, the original Confucian value of *li-zhi* was intended to develop an outstanding elite class that was both morally outstanding and capable of contributing to the society. After the Imperial Examination System was established in China, many Chinese youths set up their career aspiration as studying hard, passing the Imperial Exam, and becoming a government official. In "Three Word Chant," the concept of *li-zhi* has been expanded to include goals related to personal and family happiness, wealth, and honor. It uses vivid examples to advocate that people should set a career aspiration (ambitious career objective):[22]

- Mr. Su Laoquan (苏老泉), who didn't begin study until he was 27, but eventually became a great scholar.
- Mr. Liang Hao (梁灏), who persisted with his study and finally got the top score in the National Imperial Exam at age 82.
- Mr. Zu Ying (祖莹), who was able to compose poems when he was 8 years old.
- Mr. Li Bi (李泌), another young achiever, who was able to compose a poem to describe a chess match when he was 7.
- Mr. Liu Yan (刘晏), who was recognized as a genius and appointed as an official regarding literature when he was only 7 years old.
- Ms. Cai Wenji (蔡文姬), who became an outstanding music instrument player.
- Ms. Xie Daoyun (谢道韫), who could write beautiful poems.

By providing such extraordinary and diverse examples of individual achievement, "Three Word Chant" challenges the young: Young or old, male or female, anyone can succeed, why not you? You should set up a career aspiration and start young, obtaining the knowledge and skills you will need so you can implement them when you grow up. In this way, you will be able to serve the country, benefit your fellow citizens, bring honor to your parents and ancestors, and create wealth for your family. As "Three Word Chant" was memorized by every school student in China, the concept of *li-zhi*, determination for an outstanding life, has spread far and become deeply rooted in Chinese society.

Under centuries of Confucianism influence, the concept of *li-zhi* has become an everyday reality for every Chinese family, finding daily use in the Chinese language. In Chinese, *cheng-yu* (成语) is the most popular type of idiom, and typically it consists of four characters. Because it is very concise and easy to read and memorize, it is widely used to describe an idea, a principle, or give an analogy by way of historical example. Over the years, the Chinese have created more than 40 *cheng-yu* to describe *li-zhi*-related meanings. Every Chinese parent "w*ang- zi-cheng-long* (望子成龙) [expects his child to become a dragon, or a grand achiever]." When you are young, parents and teachers say you should have "*xiong-xin-zhuang-zhi* (雄心壮志) [be ambitious and set up your grand aspiration for your life]." They urge you to be become a "*guo-jia-dong-liang* (国家栋梁) [a pillar of the nation]" or to pursue "*rong-hua-fu-gui* (荣华富贵) [honor, glory, wealth, and noble status]." If a student is not motivated, performs poorly at school, s/he is often criticized by his/her parents as "*Xiong-wu-da-zh* (胸无大志) [having no ambition/aspiration]." If you have made a major achievement, your parents, teacher, or friends encourage you: "*Bai-chi-gan-dou, geng-jin-yi-bu* (百尺杆头，更进一步) [Congratulations on having reached the top of the 100-foot pole; please continue to make further progress]."

From these Chinese idioms you can see how strong is the Chinese people's desire to be successful!

Over the last two centuries, social and political developments have significantly changed the Chinese social structure. The Imperial Examination System was abolished in 1911. However, the Chinese never abandoned *li-zhi*, as a fundamental approach for dealing with their lives and careers. In other words, they adapted the same theme to different eras.

When China was invaded by the Japanese during World War II, many Chinese youths *li-zhi* (set up a goal) to become heroes to fight the Japanese invaders. People wrote slogans, songs, and poems to encourage young males to join the army and fight against the invaders. When communists ruled China from the 1950s to the 1970s, influenced by government propaganda, many youths set their career objective (*li-zhi*) to contribute to communism. In the late 1970s, after Deng Xiaoping implemented the Open and Reform Policy, *li-zhi* reestablished its ties with the individual and family happiness. After the college education system was restored in 1977, every family, if they were able, required that their children go to college, in particular top-ranked universities such as Peking University, Tsinghua University and University of Science and

Technology of China. After Deng Xiaoping said, "Being rich is glorious," many Chinese set up their career objectives to become entrepreneurs. Since the 1980s, a significant number of Chinese students have studied overseas and experienced many benefits of living in industrialized countries such as the US, Canada, UK, Japan, and Australia. As a result, a lot of Chinese families raised the bar for their children: Go abroad to study.

Although the modernization process did bring the Chinese people more comfort and ease of life, it did nothing to diminish their motivation. As Chinese people were exposed to better lives in Western countries, it created a sense of urgency for them to further improve their living standards. As a result, the concept of *li-zhi* has been strengthened in modern China.

In today's China, every teacher advocates his/her students to *li-zhi*, to have a grand dream, to set up a great career aspiration. It is called *you-li-xiang* (有理想) or *you-bao-fu* (有抱负) in Chinese. Every parent demands that their children study hard, go to a top-ranked university, and get a well paid job. Teachers and parents frequently recommend their students read books that encourage *li-zhi*: great leaders, great scientists, great inventors, and great entrepreneurs. As a result, the genre of *li-zhi* is among the best sellers in Chinese bookstores. Pursuing an outstanding life has become a national preoccupation across China. It was this motivation that drove the Chinese economic miracle over the last three decades and continues to drive China to further success in the future.

Obviously, other cultures embrace a similar concept of having a big dream for one's future. It is the Confucianism-influenced cultures, such as the Chinese, however, who have made it an extremely powerful motivational tool to improve their lives either in China or abroad. ***This is the first Chinese secret for success: Determination for an outstanding life!***

In the following sections, I plan to share with you how *li-zhi* is used in Confucianism-influenced Chinese families and how you can use it effectively to improve your life.

4.3 How the Chinese Use *Li-zhi* (立志) Effectively to Inspire Success

#1 Be Ambitious, Set High Aspirations for You or Your Children

Confucianism-influenced Chinese families carry their ambition, pursuit of an outstanding life, with them wherever they go. When the children are young, the parents encourage them to set ambitious objectives: Most Chinese parents typically demand their children to set a goal to go to one of the other top-ranked universities in China. For most Chinese Americans, it involves setting their sights on top schools such as Harvard, MIT, Stanford, and University of California at Berkley as their children's objectives. A high school diploma or community college degree is not even in the consideration. As pointed out by Jean Tang in a 2003 PBS documentary, *Becoming American: The Chinese Experience,* for most Chinese American families, it is not a question of whether or not to go to college. It is a question of which college to go to.[23] In the Pew Research Center Report of 2012, 27% of Asian Americans regard being successful in a high-paying career as a top priority while only 9% of the US general pubic feel the same way.[24]

Elaine Chao, the Labor Secretary under President George W. Bush, is an illustrative example. After her family emigrated to the US, her father had to work three jobs to support the family. In spite of the hardship, he supported his children to achieve their ambitious goals. He funded five of his six children's study at Harvard University, one of the best universities in the world.[25] Another example is Maya Lin, another outstanding Chinese American. Because her parents both worked at Ohio University, she could enroll there and save on tuition. However, her parents paid her tuition to enable her to go to Yale University, a more prestigious school and where she would go on to design the Vietnam War Memorial. She has been regarded as a renowned designer ever since.[26] Because many Chinese American parents have big dreams for their children, you see many Chinese faces in American's top schools such as Harvard, Yale, MIT, and Stanford.

One may argue: Why be so ambitious? Is that realistic? Why not set a less challenging goal? Not everybody can go to Harvard or MIT.

It is true that not all college-bound children can go to Harvard or MIT. The secret that many Chinese families have is to use an ambitious goal to motivate the children to reach higher. It is just like shooting at a target. If you are asked to aim at the center, 10 points, after a lot of practice, you may get good at hitting it. If not, you may end up near the center and get 8 or 9 points. If you are told that getting 5 points is enough, you will rarely try to get more than 5 points. Because many Chinese American families set Harvard or MIT as objectives for their children a good number of them end up going to Harvard or MIT whereas many others go on to attend other top-ranked schools.

Setting ambitious objectives is the first step in the pursuit of an outstanding life. It will encourage you or your children to set higher standards. It creates a reason for a person to be outstanding, not just mediocre. With such an objective, a student will not use admission into a community college as a benchmark. He or she will compete to be the best in the class or in the school and will be motivated to study harder, put forth a greater effort than other students. That student will not be likely to accept anything lower than an A.

In sports, music, and other arenas, the principle is the same. Michelle Kwan, the World Champion in Ladies Figure Skating, had an Olympic dream at an early age. It motivated her to learn and practice hard, and overcome many difficulties before finally achieving her dream.[27] Lang Lang, the world-famous Chinese pianist, had a similar story. His father discovered his musical talent when he was two years old. From that point on he was determined to make him into a world-class pianist. This aspiration motivated his family to take on many big challenges, finally enabling his success.[28]

On the contrary, if you set up a less challenging career objective, you lose the effect of motivation. If a child is expected merely to get a high school diploma or achieve an average performance in sports or music, s/he will have no incentive to study or practice harder than average. As a result, his/her potential will not be tapped. Twenty-five hundred years ago, Confucianism already had identified this important principle in the *Book of Rites*: "people's learning fails when the subject is too easy (人之学也，或失则易)."[29]

#2 Select Pragmatic Professions as Career Objectives

Setting an ambitious aspiration does not mean setting impractical objectives. It does not mean that you should follow the fashion or the spotlight cast by the pop-culture-oriented mass media.

Like many others, Chinese Americans are inundated by the pop culture and mass media of the United States. They are also exposed to coverage of sports and movie stars and overnight rags-to-riches stories such as reality TV celebrities. However, most Chinese Americans understand the chances to succeed along these career paths are relatively small because to succeed one needs some combination of extraordinary talent and luck.

Despite the exorbitant incomes of sports and movie stars, most Chinese American families do not set up their children's career objectives along these lines. If they do see their children exhibiting a talent for sports or music, Chinese parents are likely to encourage their children to pursue it and thus attain success. Representative examples are world champion figure skater Michelle Kwan, world-famous tennis player Michael Chang and NBA star Jeremy Lin. However, most Chinese families do not regard becoming a celebrity as a realistic career objective.

Influenced by the ultra-pragmatic Chinese culture, most Chinese Americans typically select career objectives in those areas that are attainable through education and hard work. It is less glorious than becoming a sports star. Such a common sense approach, however, is often overlooked by a lot of American parents. Regarding raising children in the US, we find an interesting phenomenon: Once a child reaches toddler age, a lot of non-Asian parents begin to talk about what kind of sports their child will pursue in the future. In contrast, a lot of Chinese parents begin to talk about what kind of schools their child will attend and subjects of study their child will pursue.

Chinese pragmatism is reflected not only in selecting mainstream career objectives, but also in selecting well-paid careers in high demand.

John J. Sie, founder and former Chairman and CEO of Starz Encore Group, shared his personal story during an interview with PBS in 2003. When applying to colleges in 1950s, John initially got a scholarship from Cooper Union in Manhattan, majoring in liberal arts. His father believed there was no future for a Chinese American with a liberal arts background during a time when Chinese were quite rare in the US. Because of this he encouraged him to switch his major to engineering. As a result, John turned his focus to electrical engineering, succeeded in that area, and expanded into corporate management later in his career.[30]

Today, most Chinese Americans, Korean Americans, and other Asian Americans continue this good tradition. They understand that the US needs STEM (science, technology, engineering, and math) talents. In middle school and high school science and math competitions, you see a lot of Asian participants, much higher than their percentage in the U.S. population. In America's engineering, science, and mathematics schools, you can also find high concentrations of Asian American students. They deliberately pursue the careers that the country and the market demand. It is this kind of pragmatism that helps them to obtain secure, highly paid careers for their future.

#3 Set Up Your Aspiration (Li-zhi) at an Early Age

As we discussed earlier, "Three Word Chant" uses seven examples to teach children to set up a career aspiration when they are young. It was memorized by every school student in ancient times. Today, the tradition of *li-zhi* continues. Almost every Chinese family starts to teach the child to *li-zhi* when they are in elementary school. They tell the children stories of great achievers throughout history and around the world. They want the children to believe they can be exceptional. This is similar to Western culture, in which parents fashion the daughters as princesses and the sons as little heroes.

Cherishing a child's precious childhood, keeping children innocent and treating them as princes and princesses are a worthwhile practice. It gives rise to wonderful times and memories for both children and parents. A majority of Chinese parents adopted this approach after

Western culture influenced China. In the US, we tell young children that they are princes and princesses. We tell them it is Santa Claus who brings them Christmas gifts. However, telling your children they are princesses/heroes suggests only that they deserve love and are special. It does nothing to persuade them they need to make an effort. As a result, most Chinese parents still encourage their children to *li-zhi* and to learn from great achievers after they reach elementary or early middle school age. The Chinese approach conveys a message of motivation and effort to be made. You are not born a great achiever, but you should be inspired to become one. It sets a grand goal for the children. It links the children's learning or skill development to their goals.

One may ask, when a child is young and his/her strengths and weaknesses have not yet been identified, how can a parent set up an ambitious career objective for him/her? In practice, most Chinese families handle this very skillfully. They do not set up rigid career objectives for young children. Instead, they set up ambitious, but generic goals such as going to Harvard/MIT, becoming an inventor or scientist. This creates a sense of motivation in the children, without necessarily binding them with a specifically defined, fixed objective, such as, say, to become a statistician.

After the child gains more knowledge and an understanding of society, more extensive communication will be conducted between the parents or teacher and the child. After knowing the child's strengths and their market demand, a more specific career objective can be established. As a result, *li-zhi* will be reinforced and the child's motivation for success will be strengthened.

According to scientific theory, childhood is the best time to learn. The child's brain is in a developmental stage in which education helps to shape the brain's structure and orient it to absorb knowledge effectively. For example, the best time to develop language skills is the first ten years after a child is born. If a child has not been taught any language during this period, it will be very difficult for him/her to acquire language skills later on. Clearly, the Chinese approach of setting a career aspiration at a young age makes a lot of sense. It motivates the children to learn during this valuable time window.

Also, from the lifecycle standpoint, childhood and early youth compose the golden period for learning because it is a time in which children are supported by the family and have relatively few responsibilities. If a person misses this golden period, it could make future learning more difficult. This principle was recorded in the Confucian classic, *Book of Rites,* more than 2,000 years ago. It is essential to set up a career aspiration for children when they are young.

In a poem dating back to the Tang Dynasty, the author writes "少 壮不努力，老大徒伤悲," which means: "You need to make an effort when you are young and strong. Otherwise, you will regret it when you are old." Since its publication, the phrase has become known to almost every Chinese family in the world. This phrase is even recognized by Microsoft Chinese pinyin input methods as a Chinese often-used phrase. Every Chinese parent uses this phrase to instill in their children the importance of setting up a career aspiration and making an effort at an early age. It is also used often to urge children to study hard in order to build a solid academic foundation for their future.

Obviously, it a humane and desirable way to give children a lot of love and to sustain their innocence when they are young, as most parents do in the Western societies. Nevertheless, if parents want their children to have outstanding lives, after the children reach an appropriate age, it is wise for the parents to help the children to *li-zhi*, instill in them the importance of ensuring a promising future and that they need to make an effort toward that goal. More than an expression of love, this gesture forms an important first step in preparing your children for a successful future.

This was exactly what John Sie's mother did when he was young. She told him many Chinese legends: About a poor person who worked hard and finally rose to become prime minister. About a poor kid who did not have oil for his lantern, but used fireflies as light for his study (a story cited in "Three Word Chant"). These inspiring stories helped in shaping John Sie's career aspiration and his devotion to obtaining a good education. John Sie himself cited his mother as having played an important role in laying the foundation for his career success.[31]

#4 Create Proper Parental Influences

In American society, children are given the freedom to make many choices when they are young. This practice sometimes is taken to an extreme in which there is an absence or a lack of parental influence in children's key decision making. This also is reflected in the area of setting up a career aspiration, *li-zhi*.

Some parents take a "hands off" approach, believing it is up to their children to select their own career objectives. If the child is self-motivated or motivated by peer competition (good influence by their friends/classmates), s/he will set up an ambitious career aspiration and the parents will support him/her. However, if the child is not motivated, the parents simply raise him/her to age 18, thereafter allowing him/her total control of his/her destiny.

Another situation is one in which the parents allow "what the child likes" to decide. Here the parents fully respect what the child prefers to do with his/her life. If the son is interested in engineering, the parents will support him. If the daughter likes English literature, the parents will support her regardless of the fact that the job opportunities for an English literature major may be more limited than those for a very close major, English education for non-English speakers.

The common flaw in the above two approaches lies in assuming the children's decision-making abilities are as sound as those of the adult. The truth of the matter is that, in most cases, the adult has a broader information-gathering capacity as well as a more balanced and mature decision-making ability than the children.

In addition, the second approach has another shortcoming. It assumes the child's interest is rigid, not flexible, and cannot be changed or broadened. Clearly, it is difficult to change someone from a shy, introverted person to someone who is a very sociable and outgoing. Similarly, it may be difficult to convert an accountant to a great salesperson. However, it should be no problem to help your child to change from a restrictive major to one with more job opportunities that at the same time fits his/her personality and broad interest area, for example, switching from mathematics theory to applied mathematics.

Contrary to the prevailing view of American society, a majority (66%) of Asian and Chinese Americans believe parents should have some influence over their children's career choice, in particular those who obtained a college education or higher.[32]

If ancient Confucian parenting is characterized as "the father decides everything for the children," most modern Chinese families practice a "parent guided" approach to help children to determine their career objectives. This is the approach typically taken by most Chinese American families in the US. By combining some Confucian traditions with American values on personal interests and creativity, they use the following approaches to create proper influences.

1. *Help children set up an ambitious and achievable career goal to motivate them when they are young.* The child's golden period for learning may be missed if the parents fail to act early enough.

2. *Help children to make informed decisions by bringing broad experience and a balanced perspective to the situation.* The parent can help the child to conduct research on job markets and understand:

   • Which professions have or will have good job opportunities by the time the child graduates from school,
   • Which geographic regions will offer the best job opportunities,
   • What are the skills or educational requirements needed to take advantage of such opportunities,
   • Which schools or institutes offer quality training or education for the selected profession,
   • What are the qualifications required to attend such training/education,
   • What does it cost to attain such training/education.

   Once the child has an understanding of the job market, the parents need to assist in matching his/her personal strengths and interests to the right career. Typically this involves a more sophisticated pros and cons comparison and/or cost benefit analysis. Here, I do not advocate that the parents make the precise career decisions for the children. Instead, the parents should try their best, based on their knowledge and capability, to provide more information to help the child to make informative and balanced decisions. As described earlier, that was how John Sie's father helped when John was selecting his college major. The pragmatism his father brought really changed his life, influencing his later success.

3. Help the child to make wise tradeoffs when arriving at a career decision.

In most cases, parents have more life experience and are in a position to help the child to make decisions that otherwise can be difficult for a child to handle. This is particularly true today, when children face so many diverting distractions that threaten to draw their attention away from learning. We will offer a more detailed discussion of this topic in the next section.

As a general rule, the key criterion in creating the proper influence is whether or not the parent can add value, by bringing broader knowledge or more life experience to the child's decision making. The purpose is not to advocate that parents dominate the decision making, but to help the child to make good career decisions. If you, as a parent, are not knowledgeable enough, what you should do is to get the help from your knowledgeable relatives, friends, school teachers, or colleagues. They, too, are good resources to help your children to make informed decisions. This happened to me when I was young. It also happened to many of my relatives and friends.

#5. Make an Extraordinary Effort for an Extraordinary Goal (Wise Tradeoff)

It takes extraordinary effort to achieve an extraordinary goal. Let's start with the example of pursuing a good education.

When setting up an ambitious educational aspiration, many people find it difficult to budget their time. Every person, every student has only 24 hours a day, 7 days a week. After time spent watching TV programs, playing games, and attending parties, there is not a lot of time left to prepare for college, not to mention preparing for Harvard or MIT, which are much more difficult to get accepted to.

With such limited time, it is crucial that people make wise tradeoffs. For a student, there are two choices:

A. Spend 6-8 hours more per week studying during the middle and high school years, and end up attending a first class university. The sacrifice during the middle and high school years means 6-8 hours less of playing or watching TV each week.
B. Spend 6-8 hours less per week studying, and end up attending a community college. The gain during the middle and high school years is 6-8 hours more playing or watching TV each week.

This is a tradeoff between today and the future. Here's another way to look at it: Working harder during these seven years can assure one of an increase in post-graduation income of 50% or more.

A Confucianism-influenced family will pick Choice A every time. They are willing to make a small sacrifice today in exchange for a long-lasting gain in the future. As introduced previously, *dan-bo-ming-zhi* (淡泊明志), an idiom dating back 2,000 years to the Han Dynasty, teaches those who have set career aspirations to make a sacrifice, to control today's desires in order to achieve that career aspiration. Another Chinese idiom, *zhuan-xin-zhi-zhi* (专心致志, concentrate on achieving your aspiration), clearly tells us that given time constraints, you should concentrate on achieving your aspiration for your future as opposed to engaging in other distracting activities.

After managing the time, the second challenge is the money: Getting a college degree, especially one from a top school, costs money. For many American families, if the resident state is not home to any top-ranked schools, going to one will cost even more money. This presents another difficult trade-off to be made.

Most families also have financial constraints: After paying the mortgage, food costs, auto and travel expenses, and the bill for dining out a few times each week, there is not a lot left for college tuition or other educational spending.

As I will discuss in Chapter 6, most Chinese families are willing to work hard and save money for their children's education. In the US, this is an issue that can be addressed but needs to be managed wisely.

First of all, a lot of schools offer scholarships, either merit based or non-merit based, that potentially can cover some of the cost of tuition or a stipend.

Second, a student loan program is accessible to American students and permanent residents. Attending a top school or a good graduate program ensures a better income in the future. Even if pursuing a better education means a greater initial investment, a higher future return means it is worth it.

Here, as an important warning, I do not recommend you take out a sizable loan or assume significant debt simply to attend college. There are a lot of low-quality, for-profit colleges that are interested in your enrollment and tuition but may not offer you good job prospects after you graduate. Before deciding to enroll in such a college, you need to do thorough research to determine the job prospects, such as the placement rate of graduates from these colleges. If the rates are not high, do not enroll in such a college if it means taking on debt.

In addition, people should not naively embrace the notion that a college education always leads to higher pay and a better life. It is the fit between college education and market demand that leads to higher pay and a better life, such as that which comes with highly sought after engineering, science, and math degrees. Before taking out a huge student loan, you need to conduct thorough research to find out if the major you selected correlates with high job-market demand. If not, you need to pursue a career that does in order to justify your student loan or other forms of education-related debt.

The above are two examples of wise tradeoffs in the course of pursuing a worthwhile education. You may have to make other difficult tradeoffs when you set up your other career aspirations. Pursuing extraordinary achievement in music or sports often requires much more demanding effort and sometimes investment than pursuing a good education.

Michelle Kwan, former women's figure skating world champion, is a good example of someone who has made an extraordinary effort. In order to realize her Olympic dream, she started to take skating seriously when she was eight. In the early years, she practiced three or four hours every day. Each morning, she woke up at 4:30 so she could skate before school and returned to the rink after school to skate some more. When the training and competition grew intense, Michelle and her sister Karen spent even more time in training and on the road. When their parents could no longer afford to buy them new costumes, new skates, and new skating tights, they wore homemade costumes, used secondhand skates, and shared skating tights with each other. As she described in her autobiography, *Heart of a Champion,* during her childhood, she did not have much time or the means to join the others kids in playing or having fun. But with the extraordinary effort and sacrifice she was willing to put forth, she accomplished extraordinary achievements: six-time world champion and nine-time U.S. champion in women's figure skating, a record that has never been matched by any other American.[33]

In the Asian American community, Michelle's story is not unusual. Influenced by Confucianism and other aspects of their cultural heritage, Asian Americans generally have a remarkable work ethic. According to the Pew Research Center, 69% of Asian Americans believe people can get ahead if they are willing to work hard while 58% of the American public hold the same opinion.[34]

The general principle is this: There is no easy path to success. A popular English phrase echoes this sentiment: "No pain, no gain." You have to make a choice between enjoyment or hardworking today vs. in the future. The key is to make a wise tradeoff so you will gain many more benefits overall.

#6 Make Proper Adjustments as You Grow Up

Nobody can precisely plan out his future when he is young. After having helped your son set up an aspiration to attend MIT to learn engineering, a few years down the line you may find he has better social management skills than mathematics and science skills. You may find him disinterested in college study and more drawn to entrepreneurship, similar to Steve Jobs or Michael Dell when they were young. Such a deviation from the original aspiration is beneficial because it signals your child has high-caliber aptitude although with different strengths. How do you deal with it? The answer is very straightforward: Support him in making an adjustment to an aspiration that better fits his strengths and interests. Do not force your child to pursue a career that does not utilize his/her strengths. When you support such changes, keep in mind three rules:

1. Change the aspiration, but do not lower the aspiration to a level that is not motivating or challenging.
2. Ensure the new aspiration is practical, has a realistic chance of being achieved, and leads to good job prospects.
3. Do not change the aspiration too many times. Life is short. The golden period for study is even shorter. One cannot afford to change careers too many times during his/her lifetime. If you change to a new field, you may have to start all over in your acquisition of career-related knowledge. One should not switch career paths unless the old choice does not fit you or holds no job security for the future. The older you are, the fewer career changes you should make.

In some cases, you may find the aspiration is set too high to achieve. A parent may find that despite the fact his/her child studies very hard s/he cannot maintain grades above a B. After setting up an inspirational objective to become a top-notch lawyer, for example, a student finds out that his/her logical ability is not very strong, or his/her response speed lags significantly behind that of his/her peers. Under such circumstances, it is better to adjust the career aspiration to a more achievable level. Nevertheless, it is not a good idea to adjust it downward too far, to a level that leads to a total loss of motivation.

I know from personal experience what it means to make a major career change. Like many others, I did not fully understand my true interests and strengths until I entered college. When I was in high school, I was very good at mathematics and science. I won top honors in the High School Mathematics Competition of Kunming, my hometown, which at that time had a population of about 3 million. With this achievement under my belt, I enrolled in the Department of Modern Physics at the University of Science and Technology of China, one of the country's top-ranked technology schools. At that time, my dream was to become a theoretical physicist. A few months after I arrived at the university, my physics teacher, Professor Fang Lizhi (方励之, who later became a preeminent promoter of China's democratic movement and inspired the student demonstration of 1986-87 and the Tiananmen Square Movement of 1989), gave a lecture on the future of the field. He told us that most work on theoretical physics had been accomplished, that future breakthroughs would depend largely on the ability of physics laboratories to verify hypotheses related to the fundamental structure of matter. However, conducting such experiments is increasingly expensive and difficult. In fact, there are only a few hundred people on the planet engaged in the study of theoretical physics. His honest, fact-based lecture smashed my dream of becoming a theoretical physicist. Then and there I decided to pursue another field of study and eventually discovered my interest in management. However, in the 1980s, Chinese universities were very restrictive and I could not switch my major so easily. But I did not give up. I participated in a lot of extracurricular activities related to economics and management. With this credential, after I received my Bachelor's degree in 1986 I got a job at the Institute of Policy & Management of the Chinese Academy of Sciences and started my career in industrial strategy development. If I had not made this adjustment, my career would have been much less enjoyable and rewarding to me.

Some of my classmates also made major changes after they came to the US. With exceptional academic credentials, many of them came to the US in the late 1980s, sponsored by a US-Sino Physics Education program initiated by Nobel Laureate Tsung-Dao Lee. In the course of their doctoral studies, many of them discovered their job prospects were limited. Again, Chinese pragmatism prevailed. Most of them made career changes. Some of them switched to computer science. Some of them pursued careers in the biotech field. Some became materials scientists, and some are doing quantitative modeling for Wall Street firms. All the changes they made pointed in one direction: They were made to fit their personal interests while addressing job market needs.

#7 Believe In Your Potential, Never Give Up Easily

As we discussed earlier, there is no easy path to achieving your career aspiration. The higher your ambition, the rougher the road ahead. Confucius, Mencius, and other famous Confucian scholars understood the challenges of *li-zhi*, pursuing an inspirational goal. In their minds, personal ambition and willpower are the most important of human traits. As I cited earlier, Confucius advocated determination for one's ambition: "You can kill the general in an army, but you cannot kill the ambition in a common man. (三军可夺帅也，匹夫不可夺志也)."

The determination Confucius advocated and the analogy Mencius put forth have left a deep and lasting impact on Chinese society. Chinese people are advocated to be ambitious (有志气), strive hard to be successful (奋发图强), and never give up on their aspiration (坚定不移). Many good examples can be found.

Ang Lee, the director of the Oscar-winning film *Crouching Tiger, Hidden Dragon,* emigrated to the US in 1979 from Taiwan. In order to pursue his beloved career of movie directing, he enrolled in the graduate program at the Tisch School of the Arts at New York University. During his graduate study, he won a few short-movie-directing awards. His thesis work, *Fine Line* (1984), won NYU's Wasserman Award for outstanding direction and was later selected for broadcast by PBS (Public Broadcasting Service). However, as a Taiwanese immigrant, his early career in the US was characterized by remarkable challenge. From 1984 to 1990, he was virtually unemployed. The entire family of four depended on his wife, Jane Lin, to make a living. Despite this, Ang Lee did not abandon his ambition to make movies. He continued developing movie ideas and wrote screenplays. By 1992, *Pushing Hands*, a film based on his screenplay and directed by Ang Lee, achieved huge success in Taiwan. As a result, his film-directing career started taking off. Today, he is the most successful Chinese American movie director in the world.[35]

Michelle Kwan's pursuit of her figure-skating career was also fraught with challenge during the early days of her training. She grew up in a middle class family, and her parents had a modest income. Like many other Chinese American parents, they devoted all their effort and money to supporting Michelle and her sister Karen in the pursuit of their dreams to become world champions. The two sisters reached a point in the development of their skating skills that they needed more skating-rink time. This led to financial hardship with their family. In order to make ends meet, their mother took on a second job and their father worked extra hours to finance the rink time and coaching fee. Eventually, their parents had to sell their house, and moved the family to live with their grandparents for several years. When Michelle was ten years old, her family could no longer afford a coach. At one point, she did not have a coach for nine months and had to practice on her own. At such critical times, a few kind friends who appreciated her talent provided a helping hand, offering her financial assistance to help her continue training. Such examples make it clear her parents' resolve and commitment to support her training were extraordinary. With such parental devotion, coupled with her extraordinary training, it finally paid off. In 1994, she won the World Junior Championship, and later the 1996 World Championship. This was just the beginning of an amazing career; she would go on to win many U.S. and world championships in the years to come.[36]

Ang Lee and Michelle Kwan provide outstanding examples of Chinese Americans who are resilient, and up to the challenge. Their stories are not the exception. In the Chinese American community, you can find many stories like theirs, in particular from first generation immigrants. In order to survive in the US, they have had to overcome the language barrier, culture shock, and in many cases, financial difficulties. Pursuing the American Dream presents an enormous challenge to them. But with their fortitude, willpower, and positive attitude they are able to succeed: They rarely take things for granted. They believe in self-reliance. They believe that hard work will yield good results. Based on this belief, they are willing to make an extra effort in order to realize their American Dreams.

Chapter 5.

SECOND VALUE: *QIN-XUE* (勤学)

"Pursuing an Excellent Education"— Confucian Value on Achieving a Successful Life in a Most Reliable Way

5.1 WHY EDUCATION IS ESSENTIAL FOR PURSUING A HAPPY LIFE IN TODAY'S SOCIETY

As we discussed earlier, American education is no longer on top. Today it lags behind many industrialized nations and Asian countries in particular in the areas of math and science education. More and more politicians, educators, responsible news anchors, and journalists have started to emphasize the importance of education to the future of the US and to the future lives of individual Americans. After the PISA 2009 report was released, the U.S. Secretary of Education, Arne Duncan, said: "But the findings, I'm sorry to report, show that the United States needs to urgently accelerate student learning to remain competitive in the knowledge economy of the 21st century... Americans need to wake up to this educational reality—instead of napping at the wheel while emerging competitors prepare their students for economic leadership."[1]

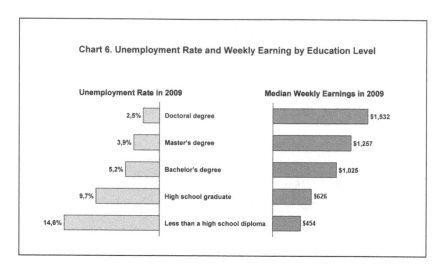

Chart 6. Unemployment Rate and Weekly Earning by Education Level

What is the role of education with regard to people's economic wellbeing—employment and income? The answer is clear: Education pays! The above is a chart based on 2009 data from the Bureau of Labor Statistics.[2] On the income side, in 2009 a typical college graduate earned 63% more per week than someone with only a high school diploma. A person with a Master's or Doctoral degree earned even more, on average 2 and 2.45 times the salary of a high school graduate, respectively.

People with higher education also have a lower unemployment rate. In 2009, the unemployment rate for people who lacked a high school diploma was the highest: 14.6%. Those with a high school diploma had a rate of 9.7%. For people with a college degree or higher, the unemployment rate dropped significantly—only 5.2% for those with a Bachelor's degree, 3.9% for those with a Master's degree, and 2.3% for those with a Doctoral degree. Today's job market points clearly in one direction: A good education leads to a high employment rate and a higher salary.

Can most Americans maintain a good life without good education in the future? The answer is: No! There are a few compelling reasons every American needs to know:

1. The rapid evolution of technology has led to more and more jobs becoming knowledge based

Throughout human history, a clear trend has emerged: The advancement of technology changes people's daily life and the way they work. After the tractor was invented in 1892, it proved much faster and more powerful than horses and water buffalos for plowing fields. In order to acquire the improved capacity for productivity made possible by utilizing tractors, farmers had to abandon their old skills of raising and operating horses or water buffalos, and learn the new skills of operating and maintaining machinery, which required minimal reading skills and some knowledge of mechanics. This is an example of a technology-driven job transformation process.

The 20th century saw the rapid advancement of science and technology, including the invention of the airplane, the television, the computer, the Internet, and other revolutionary technologies. It also accelerated the job transformation process. In high-tech areas, the designers of the iPhone would need to understand electronics technology, telecommunications technology, computer technology, and cutting edge nanotechnology. Even in traditional industries such as auto repair, technology content is increasing. In the past, a working knowledge of mechanics and electronics was sufficient to handle most auto repair work. Today, with many computer and control technologies being incorporated into the manufacturing of automobiles, auto repair technicians have to learn to operate computerized diagnostic systems. The trend is obvious: Increasingly more jobs will become knowledge based, which will require a good education as a basic job requirement. According to a survey of 600 executives as a part of a business roundtable commission known as the Springboard Project, "two thirds of employers surveyed say they require at least an associate's college degree for most positions."[3] With continued technology advancement, the educational requirements could become even higher in the future.

2. Global competition is reducing low-knowledge-content manufacturing and services in advanced countries

As we discussed in Chapter 1, the last half of the 20th century, in particular following the establishment of the World Trade Organization (WTO) in 1995, saw an acceleration in globalization. As a result, the trade barriers between countries have been reduced significantly. Since 2000, over six million American manufacturing jobs have been lost, most of them to low-cost countries such as China and Mexico. In addition to the loss of manufacturing jobs, the borderless service platform created by modern telecommunications and Internet technologies has enabled massive service outsourcing, transferring millions of U.S. service jobs such as call center jobs to India and the Philippines.

In addition to such "legal" competition, Americans are also faced with "illegal" competition from undocumented immigrants. Illegal immigrants typically are willing to take significantly lower paying jobs as long as it is more than they can earn in their home country. Unfortunately, this situation exacerbates the job dilemma for Americans who have the least education. As the 2009 data makes clear, Americans who lack a high school diploma have the highest unemployment rate at 14.6%.

With such international competition, low-knowledge-content job opportunities in the US are declining. When the demand for such jobs is much less than the supply, the corresponding salaries decline. The conclusion is straightforward: If you do not obtain sufficient knowledge and skills to keep up with the requirements for good jobs, you will be left to choose from low-income jobs and may have difficulty finding any job in the long run.

3. Education has become essential for dealing with life decisions

When considering an education, most people typically focus on the job-attainment side. Good education leads to a good job. Quite often people forget to think about the importance of an education in helping them deal with daily life decisions.

In a modern society like the US, people encounter many important decisions that require the application of sound knowledge and judgment. Let's just list a few items essential to achieving the American Dream:

a) Buying and financing a house. Buying a house typically is the most expensive decision you will make. You will need to consider location, school zone, house layout, and price, among other things. There are no simple ratings systems to tell you which one is the best after taking into account all your criteria. After days of comparison and assessment, most people are able to come to a decision on their dream house. However, recent history reveals that many Americans failed during the financing process. Partially because of the greed of bankers/mortgage sellers and partially because of a lack of mathematics/financing knowledge, many Americans chose an adjustable rate or other type of high-risk mortgage, landing themselves in financial hot water. Too many of them ended up losing their beloved homes. By comparison, I hear of few Chinese Americans who have fallen into such traps. What made the difference is education—mathematics and financial knowledge.

b) Buying and financing a car. In choosing a car, you need to find something that fits your needs and your budget. You want make a good decision. A lot of factors need to be considered: make, reliability, gas mileage, etc. Most Americans may have little difficulty in making a selection. Again, the more difficult part for the average American is the financing. Do you understand how much the dealer really charges you and the ramifications of all the written and hidden charges? In 1996, I encountered a dealer who said he could offer me a car loan with 7% interest rate. After I got home, I calculated that the actual interest rate was at 9% based on the total loan amount and monthly payment number he gave to me. When confronted by my facts, he told me a hidden service fee had been added to the financing. I walked away from this dealer and never went back.

Again, knowledge can help you avoid being taken advantage of by predatory lenders.

c) Managing your retirement fund. This will involve investment skills. If you lack a high school education, the odds of you being able to control your investment funds are minimal.

d) Selecting a good career for you or your children. This will require a good understanding of the job market as well as the interests and strengths of you or your children. Many times, this is not an easy task. You have to conduct research, and sometimes get the opinion of outside experts. If your knowledge is limited, you will have difficulty reaching sound decisions. The list goes on. An unavoidable fact is that Americans live in a knowledge-driven and complex society. Everybody needs sufficient knowledge to ensure s/he has a good life and does not fall into hazardous situations. How do you get the needed knowledge? A good education!

If you combine the three factors discussed above, it is easy to see that the level of education you get determines two different paths for your life:

Chart 7. Different Paths of Life Determined by Education

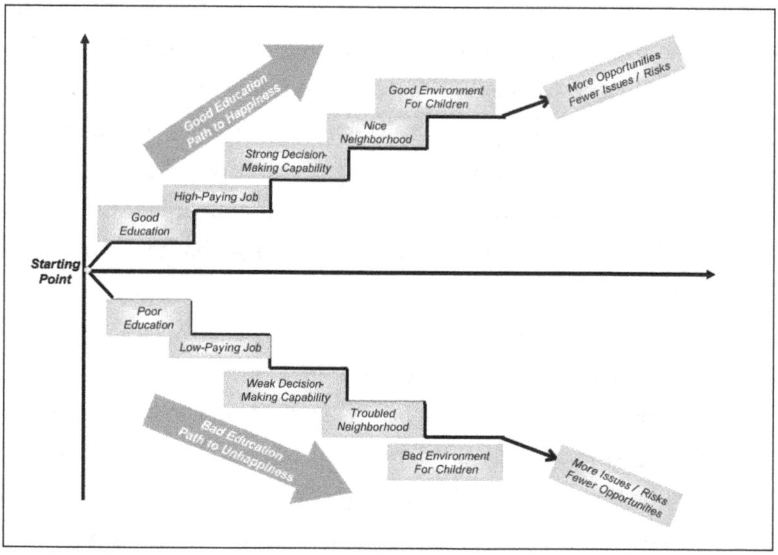

The first path, a good education (graduate from a respectable college with marketable skills), goes to a virtuous circle: With a good education you are likely to get a high-paying job, live in a nice neighborhood, and be capable of dealing with major financial decisions such as buying a house and managing your investments. Your children are likely to grow up in a safe neighborhood with good schools and have a chance at a good education. Your family is likely to run a low risk of being negatively impacted by drug abuse and other bad influences. This is a virtuous circle that brings you and your children a good life.

The second path, poor education (high school dropout), goes to a vicious circle: With a poor education you are likely get a low-paying job, run a higher risk of unemployment, live in a less desirable neighborhood, be unable to deal with major life decisions, be more likely to be cheated by greedy bankers and other predators, and have little chance to save for your retirement. Your children are likely to grow up in an unsafe neighborhood and run the risk of involvement with drugs and crime, which will give you cause for worry every day of your parenting life. This is a vicious circle that many people want to get out of.

Between these two paths, a Confucianism-influenced family will always pick the first one—pursuing a good education—no matter how poor the family is.

5.2 The Confucian Value of *Qin-xue* (勤学): Pursuing an Excellent Education

If you want to name one value that most distinguishes Chinese culture, it is emphasizing education. It is also one of the biggest influences Confucius and his followers had on Chinese society. As I introduced in Chapter 3, Confucius said he set his personal aspiration (*li-zhi*) on learning when he was 15 years old. He described himself as a persistent learner who never lost his interest in learning (学而不厌). He regarded learning as one of the most important ways to acquire the knowledge of the world (人不学，不知道)[4] and advocated that people strive to learn. About 2,500 years ago, Confucius started the first recorded private school in China. He trained about 3,000 disciples, 72 of whom became distinguished politicians, administrators, and scholars. His disciples continued opening schools and spreading Confucian philosophies. As a result, Confucians became a lasting force in expanding education in China.

In addition to championing the power of knowledge and leading the education expansion of ancient China, Confucianism developed many rich educational principles and methods. In particular, in the *Book of Rites,* there is a chapter dedicated to learning. It records many wise and effective education approaches.

1. ***Childhood is the best time to learn.*** Initiated by Mencius and cited in "Three Word Chant," Confucianism established the concept of "Study the knowledge when you are young; apply the knowledge after you grow up (幼而学，壮而行)."[5] The *Book of Rites* professes the same principle (大学之法…当其可之谓时) and emphasizes if a person misses the best time—childhood—to learn, learning will be more difficult during adulthood.[6]

2. ***The best education is to maintain a student's interest in learning.*** The *Book of Rites* says, A good teacher is one who can keep and encourage a student's interest in learning (善教者，使人继其志).[7] This is a very important concept. In order to maintain a student's interest in learning, a teacher needs to make learning as a journey both enjoyable and challenging. This includes maintaining an appropriate degree of difficulty and study load, and keeping a good balance between study and play.

3. ***Progress should be based on a student's aptitude and learned knowledge.*** The *Book of Rites* says one of the key successful teaching methods is to base progress on a student's aptitude and learned knowledge (大学之法…不凌节而施之为孙).[8] It emphasizes a systematic, step-by-step approach: Educate the student with fundamental knowledge first. After the student

has sufficiently assimilated the prerequisite knowledge, progress to a higher level.

4. ***Stimulate students' thinking instead of coercing or just memorizing the knowledge.*** Confucius emphasized the importance of thinking (思) in the process of learning (学). He said: "Learning without thinking leads to confusion; thinking without learning leads to failure (学而不思则罔，思而不学则殆)."[9] He also initiated the elicitation method of teaching 2,500 years ago. Similarly, the *Book of Rites* also advises that teachers use induction and other methods to stimulate learning rather than coercing students to learn.

5. ***Group learning and knowledge sharing.*** The *Book of Rites* promotes group learning and knowledge sharing as an effective way to broaden knowledge and encourage learning from one another (大学之法…相观而善之谓摩).[10]

6. ***Prevent bad behavior from taking place.*** In addition to propagating knowledge Confucianism also stresses moral education. As described in the *Book of Rites* (大学之法，禁于未发之谓预), its focus is on forestalling bad behavior.[11]

The Confucian value of emphasizing education and its many wise educational methods have established a good foundation for educational advancement in ancient China. It was the establishment of the Imperial Examination System that made education a national passion in China. As mentioned in Chapter 3, about 1,500 years ago, Sui Wendi, the first emperor of the Sui Dynasty, formally established the world's first Imperial Examination System on a nationwide scale for the purpose of selecting government officials through national examination. Since the adoption of the Imperial Examination System, education has become the main avenue for Chinese to pursue good careers and realize their upward mobility. The "Ancient Chinese Dream" of becoming a well paid and highly respected government official has motivated tens of millions of Chinese youths to study hard since ancient times. Every Chinese, if given the chance, would make every effort to pursue this dream.

"Three Word Chant," the secular bible of Confucianism, further promotes the importance of education. Out of about 1,000 characters, it uses more than 200 to teach young students the importance of education and hard study. It describes 14 examples showing how a person succeeded through diligent study. Following are a few well known Chinese examples that demonstrate the extraordinary study ethics and willpower exhibited by those people:[12]

- Mr. Che Yun (车胤) of the Jin (晋) Dynasty. His family was too poor to afford an oil lamp. In order to study, he collected fireflies to light his reading at night.
- Mr. Sun Kang (孙康) of the Jin (晋) Dynasty. His family was also too poor to afford an oil lamp. In order to study, he used the light reflected from the snow for his reading.
- Mr. Li Mi (李密) of the Tang (唐) Dynasty. His family was also too poor to send him to school. In order to learn, he tied a book to the horn of one of the bulls he herded and read whenever he had time.
- Mr. Sun Jing (孙敬) of the Jin (晋) Dynasty. He tied his hair to the roof beam while he studied late at night. This prevented him from nodding off.
- Mr. Su Qin (苏秦) of the Warring States (战国) period. When he stayed up to study, he used a needle to poke his leg to prevent himself from falling asleep.

These stories provide a glimpse into how the expectations attached to education and study ethics in ancient Chinese society were very high. In addition, the standards were restrictive. If a student was late to school or lazy in class, he would be caned by his teacher. If he failed to perform academically, he would be caned at home by his father. On the other hand, good behavior and good performance were always encouraged by the teacher and the parents.

Throughout their history, Chinese people have associated education and knowledge with making a good living and pursuing a successful career. The social/economic changes of the last few centuries in China may have reset the priorities of the Chinese people temporarily. However, the Chinese people have never wavered in their belief that education is the most important thing to a family. For example, my sister, brother, and I grew up during the Cultural Revolution, which turned out to be a cultural demolition. During this period, college education in China ceased for 10 years, from 1966 to 1976, and all the intellectuals were persecuted politically. Nevertheless, my parents, who had only an elementary and middle school education, still encouraged us to study hard and perform well academically. Although it went against the Maoist doctrine, many schoolteachers took a huge personal risk and taught students in secret about the importance of knowledge and education.

In 1977, college education was restored, one year after Mao Zedong died. Ever since then, the National College Entrance Examination has become as revered as the Imperial Examination in the past. The difference is this: The National College Entrance Examination throws open the doors to many professions such as engineering, management, law, government service, and the healthcare professions while the Imperial Examination only provided a single career channel to become a government official. As a result, it is the goal of almost every Chinese family to enable their child to pass the National College Entrance Exam and be admitted into a college, preferably an excellent one. In today's China, education continues to be a national passion for almost all Chinese families.

In the last few decades, pop culture also invaded China at a rapid speed, swaying many youths to start worshipping sports stars, movie stars, and other celebrities. Nevertheless China remains a knowledge-centric, education-focused society. In China, scientists and academic experts are highly respected. Their influence on national policy and social issues is much stronger than that of sports or movie stars. The elected members (selected based on career achievements) of the Chinese Academy of Sciences, Chinese Academy of Social Sciences, and Chinese Academy of Engineering are almost as influential as the CEOs of major corporations. They frequently give advice on Chinese economic or technology policymaking. College and graduate degrees are both prerequisite for many positions and an indication of social status. Many successful CEOs still spend time in pursuing a Ph.D. degree in management through part-time study. Zhao Wei, a leading Chinese actress, after becoming a super-famous and super-rich movie star, still devoted two years to studying and received her Master's degree. A similar story describes what happened to Michelle Kwan, a Chinese American. After retiring from figure skating, she enrolled in the University of Denver, graduating in 2009. Two years later, she completed her Master's degree in Law and Diplomacy from Tufts University, laying a good foundation for her career transition.

Most modern Chinese families, whether they live in China or overseas, inherit the good Confucian tradition of appreciation of the power of knowledge. They view education as the first priority for the family. They also apply many Confucian educational principles and methods to enhance their education. A lot of them have done quite well to help their children to achieve excellent educations. As a result, in the US, over 50% of Chinese Americans have received a college degree or higher. *This is the second Chinese secret for success: Pursuing an excellent education is the most reliable way to achieve a successful life.*

In the following section, I am going to share with you how *qin-xue* (pursuing an excellent education) is accomplished in Confucianism-influenced Chinese families and how they use many Confucian education methods to achieve this goal successfully.

5.3 How *Qin-Xue* (勤学) Is Accomplished in Chinese Families to Achieve an Excellent Education

#1 Become Educational Parents

According to Confucianism, parents have the inescapable responsibility to educate the children. "Three Word Chant" clearly states this important point: "It is the father's fault if he only raises but not educates the child (养不教，父之过)."[13] It cites the story of Mr. Dou Yan Shan (窦燕山).[14] He successfully educated his five sons, and all of them passed the Imperial Exams and became famous. It also tells the story of the mother of Mencius. She took a very active role in educating his son when he was young. One day, when Mencius was reciting an essay, his memory failed him and he stopped in the middle. Upon seeing this, his mother stopped her work and cut the cloth she was weaving in half. She told Mencius of the importance of assimilating knowledge as a whole and compared it to weaving a cloth. As you will read in Chapter 7, she also took more dramatic measures in her effort to educate Mencius. As a result, she is one of the most famous parenting role models in Chinese history.[15]

In Confucianism-influenced Chinese families, all parents devote time, money, and effort to their children's education. If the parents are knowledgeable, they directly participate in shaping the learning, wisdom, and moral characters of their children. For example, Zhu Guo Liang (诸葛亮) of the Three Kingdom Period, Zeng Guo Fan (曾国藩), an outstanding general of the Qing Dynasty who defeated the rebellion of the Taiping Heavenly Kingdom, and Fu Lei (傅雷), a preeminent 20th century Western literature translator who introduced many classical Western novels to China, all have left inspiring essays and books to guide the rearing of their children. If the parents are not educated, they still pay close attention to their children's academic progress and provide timely support with their education.

David Ho, the outstanding AIDS researcher, told his personal story in an interview with PBS in 2003. When he was six, his father left the family in Taiwan to pursue higher education in the US. Due to financial constraints, for many years he could not bring them to the US or even call them regularly. Having foreseen such a difficult time, when he left Taiwan, he gave his wife, David's mother, only one instruction: Make sure the kids are well educated.[16]

His story is not alone. If you read any outstanding Chinese American biography—Maya Lin, John Sie, Jerry Yang, Andrea Jung, Gary Locke, Elain Chao—all attribute their success to their parents' devotion to their education. All of my relatives and Chinese American friends are such parents. They view giving their children the best education possible as a parent's most sacred responsibility. This is a common theme and the norm in Chinese society.

In Chinese culture, education is not the sole responsibility of the student and the teacher. The parents are the champions, the mentors and service providers for the children's education. What they do is much more than just turning off the TV when their children are studying. They take an active role in every step of their children's education: After a child is born, the parents start buying books, CDs for beginners and preschoolers. They start to teach the children English letters, numbers, Chinese characters, and poems. They tell the children inspiring stories and help them set up a career aspiration. After the children start school, they demand high academic standards and monitor the children's progress. They reward the children for their good academic performance and pressure the children to improve if they show unsatisfactory progress. If the children are not at the top of the class, they will tutor the children themselves or send the children to tutoring schools. They also spend a significant amount of time to send the children to learn Chinese, English, music, and sports. In Chinese culture, one generation's success is typically built on two generations' efforts—their parents' and their own.

#2 Nurture a Family Culture That Appreciates Knowledge and Education

Among all the influences children are exposed to during their school years, family culture is typically the most important. Hard-working parents tend to raise hard-working children. Well-behaved parents have a high chance of raising kids that are behaved. The same logic applies with respect to knowledge and a passion for education.

If the parents fixate on the shallow aspects of pop culture (such as movie-star gossip, the personal lives of famous athletes) and pay no respect to successful thinkers—engineers, scientists, and scholars—their children are very likely to follow suit. The children are unlikely to show respect to their teachers and listen to their instructions. If children are showered with nothing but toys and games as opposed to books, it sends a message that playing is more important than learning.

Chinese society is one that worships knowledge, wisdom, and education. It is the birthplace of many great strategists such as Suntzu, author of *The Art of the War*. Many historical novels and stories such as *The Three Kingdoms* are filled with political and military wisdom and strategy. Even in today's China, when good-looking girls pick their boyfriends, a boy's education, knowledge, and wisdom very often carry more weight than his looks. This is in clear opposition to the United States, where boys' athletic prowess and physical strength are often what girls focus on.

Living in such a culture, most Chinese people deeply believe having good knowledge/skills leads to a good life and the best way to obtain good knowledge/skills is through good education. They have strong motivation to enable their children to get a good education. Unlike in the US, where academically successful kids often are labeled as "nerds," being knowledgeable and smart are valued highly in most Chinese families and schools. This sends a clear message to parents to guide and motivate their children to obtain a good education.

The same thing is happening in Chinese American communities. In the 2003 PBS documentary, *Becoming American: The Chinese Experience*, Jean Tang described the education-centric culture in Chinatown. At home, her parents asked them to study hard, get excellent grades. Outside the home, the children's education remained the parents' focus. During the weekend, her parents, owners of a small retail store, frequently had parties with the owners of other Chinese stores and restaurants, playing mahjong together. At these parties, they rarely talked about business matters. Instead, they talked about their children. They shared stories about how one family's child was accepted to a top university or another family's child received an award at school. All the parents were very proud of what their children had achieved academically. They were very eager to learn about the successful parenting experiences of other parents. With such passion and devotion from her parents along with the personal effort she put forth, Jean Tang was accepted by Stanford University and graduated with the top 1% of students.[17]

Chinese families also pay great respect to teachers, in particular those teachers who can help their children to improve. In the *Book of Rites,* Confucianism states: "If the teacher is respected, the knowledge is respected, and then people will value the learning (师严然后道尊，道尊然后民知敬学)." In the US, if a child receives a grade that does not meet the parents' expectations, the parents may challenge the teacher for her strict grading approach. If this happens in Chinese society, the parents typically take the opposite approach: They may send gifts to the teacher, begging the teacher to spend more time with their child to help them to learn more and therefore improve their test scores. Respecting one's teacher is another essential cultural element that creates a proper relationship between teacher and student and makes teachers' efforts more easily accepted by children.

After 18 years of living in the US, I have started seeing some encouraging signs. On October 18, 2010, President Obama hosted a White House Science Fair, celebrating the winners of a broad range of science, technology, engineering, and math (STEM) competitions. Coming from the President of the United States, this gesture sends a very important message: Education and technology matter. As President Obama put it, "If you win the NCAA championship, you come to the White House. Well, if you're a young person and you produce the best experiment or design, the best hardware or software, you ought to be recognized for that achievement, too… in many ways our future depends on what happens in those (science and technology) contests."[18]

For those parents who want their children to get a good education and have a successful future, you need to examine your family culture: Does it respect or disrespect education/knowledge? You need to be aware that parents are the most important role model for their children. If you do not value knowledge, disrespect teachers, and indulge in celebrity gossip, it will be more difficult for your children to be motivated to pursue a good education. If you already have or intend to create a family culture that values knowledge and emphasizes education, it will help your children's education tremendously.

#3 Set up High Standards for Your Children

As discussed in Chapter 4, setting a great ambition is an effective approach to motivate your children. It is essential for children to have a great career aspiration, to pursue outstanding lives.

A great goal, if it lacks the means to assess progress toward it, will end up in futility. To support such a goal, parents need to set up high standards for the children, especially considering today's U.S. public education system, which has lost its way in living up to reasonable academic standards.

As I cited in Chapter 4, in 1990, the Office of Educational Research and Improvement of the U.S. Department of Education held a national conference on student motivation. At the conference, researchers pointed out an unhealthy trend in the US: lowering education standards. They listed the following reasons:[19]

- "In their attempt to be fair and to protect their pupils' self-esteem, teachers often excuse disadvantaged children from the effort that learning requires. This practice obscures the connection between effort and accomplishment and shields children from the consequences. The practice also sets the stage for later failure."

- "To increase graduation rate, some schools have allowed students to design their own courses of study, offered credit for less-rigorous alternatives to core subjects, and awarded diplomas to students who merely stayed in the courses and accumulated credits... Similarly, the need to demonstrate academic achievement as a prerequisite for entering college has given way to the belief that any high school student who wants to go to college should not be denied the opportunity." As a result, "Graduation rates have gone up, achievement scores have gone down."

- "Educational researchers note an increase in teacher-student "bargains," those usually tacit but sometimes explicit agreements in which teachers lower their standards in exchange for classroom cooperation."

As a result, teachers are too lenient in their grading, handing out too many As and naming too many honor roll students, regardless of whether or not the students actually learned and mastered the subject matter.

It has been more than 20 years since the national conference on student motivation took place. However, the situation has not changed significantly. In 2001, Mareen Staut, a professor of education at California State University, published a provocative book, *The Feel-Good Curriculum: The Dumbing Down of America's Kids in the Name of Self-Esteem*.[20] In it she lists many detrimental effects of the "self-esteem movement" on American public education, in particular the dropping American educational standards. She points out that when teachers and children put personal feelings above proper evaluation, testing becomes easier and students learn less. Nine years later, Robert Samuelson wrote in his column, "School reform's meager results," on September 6, 2010: "Since the 1960s, waves of 'reform' haven't produced meaningful achievement gain."[21] According to 2012 ACT test results, only one out of four participants (high school graduates) met four key benchmarks and is ready for college.[22]

Why is that? It is primarily because of the low standards used in American schools. Let me give you an example I uncovered while tutoring my kids for a mathematics competition. In a typical school in China, following instruction in math the teacher requires students to solve eight problems: the first four are used to gauge the student's understanding of the principle; the second four are used to gauge the student's memorization of the principle. With talented students, they will add two more problems to further challenge and develop their skills. In comparison, a typical American math teacher gives students only four problems to solve. Even if the student solves them correctly, which is not always the case, it merely helps the student in understanding the principle, not in memorizing it. Different standards and different study loads clearly lead to different results.

On November 16, 2010, *ABC News* described a Chinese mother, Jane Feng, who sent her 16-year-old son to the US as preparation for him applying to U.S. colleges. Jane said that when her son was in China, his grades were average. After he came to the US, however, he immediately became a math superstar.[23] Theirs is not a unique story. I personally know many Chinese Americans who brought their school-age children to the US. After overcoming the language barrier all of them became top performers in their classes. One German colleague told me a similar story. His brother, an 11th grader in Germany, was transferred to an American school for study. As soon as he started taking classes, he found the 11th grade curriculum was not challenging enough for him. As a result, he immediately advanced to the 12th grade and gradated with straight As. The conclusion such anecdotes point to is this: American educational standards are too low, in comparison with China and many other countries.

In particular, the American educational standards on science and math are too low to educate sufficiently high-skilled workers to meet the needs of the country's high-tech firms. In April 2011, a group of executives calling itself "Change the Equation" warned that "if States do not set a meaningful bar for assessing these skills (science and math), they risk contributing to the dilution of America's global competitiveness," according to a May 20, 2011, *Fortune Magazine* report.[24]

Because American public education does not live up to the standards it should, it fails to produce a sufficient labor force in terms of both quantity and quality, in particular in the high-tech areas. Consequently, as mentioned in Chapter 4, a lot of engineering-driven American companies have to hire educated immigrants, who in many cases have come to form the backbone of their engineering departments.

In many American public schools, 20-30% of children are awarded As, regardless of whether or not they have truly mastered the subject. The quality of the A grade has been significantly diluted. Leading universities will accept only the top 5% of students. For the parents of a B student, the chances of their child being accepted to a top school is very slim.

Recognizing the shortcomings of the American public school system, most Chinese American parents will not accept Bs or lower grades from their children. This is because that they understand that B grades indicate a level of learning that is insufficient to prepare their children for a secure and promising future. What they expect of their children is a thorough understanding of the subject matter. This is essential to building an academic foundation solid enough to allow the children to graduate from one grade level to the next.

In order to prepare their children for the future, many Chinese American and Asian American families do not stop at an A-level academic performance. They encourage their children to participate and excel in standard tests because it reflects a consistent standard statewide. Most enroll their children in the Advanced Placement (AP) Program or the International Baccalaureate Program, which offers higher educational standards than regular American high schools. They also want their children to learn more and at a younger age. According to research conducted by the Higher Education Research Institute in January 2010, 33.8% of Asian American high school students take 5-9 AP classes vs. 15.4% for White Americans and 18.9% for Hispanic Americans.[25] Again, the data indicate that Asian American students are held to higher academic standards.

In addition to academics, most Chinese American families ask the children to learn foreign languages and musical instruments. They ask the children to participate in various competitions and student clubs: math, science, Beta Clubs, etc. They encourage them to excel not only in school, but in county, state, and even national competitions. Enabling your children to become top performers helps create in them a true sense of self-esteem and pride, a sense of self-appreciation for his/her excellent ability. It motivates children to continue to perform exceptionally.

This process not only helps build children's confidence and skills, but it also opens more doors to their career development, more opportunities to be accepted by top universities, recognized and accepted by top-notch coaches, and trained in a specific area such as music, sports, and the arts.

Some readers may ask: If the standards are set so high, will children have the time and ability to achieve them?

Parents who have no experience of living abroad generally believe that if their children attend classes and complete their homework, this is enough study. But they may not realize that American students are among those who spend the least time studying. Take the example of the public school my children attend. Each year they go to school for 170 days. Each day they have about six hours of study except for Wednesday, when they study for only five hours. For the year this amounts to 950-1000 hours, about 50% of the hours worked by the average American employee.

According ABC News, Chinese students spend at least 41 more days a year in the classroom than American students. They spend longer hours doing homework than American students.[26] In a less demanding environment, Japanese students spend twice the amount of time doing homework than American students.

The ugly truth is that American students have become accustomed to lower educational standards and fewer study hours. Many of them will at some point in the future find themselves competing either directly or indirectly (such as company outsourcing) with Chinese, Japanese, Korean, and European workforces that are trained with higher standards and longer study hours. If foreign laborers offer better skills at equal or less pay, companies cannot resist the appeal to relocate factories and even R&D centers to those countries. As I pointed out in Chapter 1, this is the sort of job loss that has been happening in the US since the late 20th century.

#4 Be Reasonably Strict; Do Not Raise Your Children as "Indoor Flowers"

In early 2011, I watched a remarkable documentary on the History Channel: *America: The Story of Us.*[27] It depicts several moving accounts drawn from American history: How George Washington led the Continental Army, overcoming almost insurmountable difficulties—

lack of military supply, contentious disease, and a brutal winter—to finally prevail against the British. How pioneers conquered rugged mountains and harsh weather to finally settle the West. How Thomas Edison, after endless trial and error, finally invented the electric light bulb. What these stories demonstrate is a spirit of resilience and endurance in a people that were up to whatever challenge life had in store for them.

Perhaps because the US has since grown into an affluent society and life has become easier for her citizens, over the decades, many American parents gradually have become lenient with their children. Some modern psychology theories have persuaded many parents to focus on their children's self-esteem and to avoid challenging them on their academic progress. In addition, many parents are advised by popular "experts" and talk show hosts to avoid hurting their children's feelings and to respect their children's choices regardless of the child's capacity to make reasonable choices. Equally significant, the parents' key mission has become to maintain a good relationship with their children and to give them love and care, instead of preparing them with sufficient knowledge and skills for their future.

Unfortunately, these modern psychological doctrines have created some undesirable consequences: reducing the individual and parents' sense of responsibility and discipline. As a result, many children were raised as "indoor flowers," unequipped to withstand the sunlight, wind, and rains of a natural environment. Parents are reluctant to demand good performance from their children. Many children are not required to devote themselves to after-school study and to completing their homework. What is the consequence? Children are discouraged from working hard. As pointed out by researchers, "Children 'read' sympathy offered to them when they fail, praise proffered for very modest accomplishments, and help tendered when it is unsolicited as signs that they lack ability."[28] Such an overly protective style of parenting fails to help children establish a vital study ethic. Consequently many of them fail in school and/or later in their careers.

As cited in Chapter 4, in 2006, Patrick Welsh, an English teacher at T. C. Williams High School in Alexandria, Virginia, pointed out in his commentary in *USA Today*: "Kids who had emigrated from foreign countries—such as Shewit Giovanni from Ethiopia, Farah Ali from Guyana and Edgar Awumey from Ghana—often aced every test, while many of their U.S.-born classmates from upper-class homes with highly educated parents had a string of C's and D's.... What many of the American kids I taught did not have was the motivation, self-discipline or work ethic of the foreign-born kids."[29]

The bigger tragedy characterizing today's America is this: Many parents are not aware of the competition their children face from those children with a stricter, more disciplined educational background. They staunchly believe the US is number 1 in the world and the American approach is always the best approach. Gradually, they have lost sight of sound American traditions and lost ground to countries with more disciplined approaches to education, such as Singapore, Korea, China, Finland, and other industrial nations. This view is widely shared by Asian Americans. According to a 2012 Pew Research Center Report, "62% of Asian Americans believe most American parents do not put enough pressure on their children to do well in school."[30]

In Confucianism-influenced families, it is expected that parents and teachers be strict with students in regard to their learning and their behavior. In "Three Word Chant," it says, "It is the teacher's fault if students are not taught strictly and responsibly (教不严，师之惰)."[31] The concept that a "strict teacher gives rise to outstanding disciples (严师出高徒)" is a widely accepted education concept in China. In this approach, children are often required to push themselves hard. With disciplined effort, they eventually accomplish tasks that they once thought were beyond their ability. This is the approach that has produced many exceptional acrobats, gymnastics, and other great achievers. It also illustrates the endurance many Chinese students demonstrate during their study.

Yo-Yo Ma, fifteen-time Grammy Award winner and one of the best cellists in the world, is another beneficiary of strict parenting, in this case from his father, Dr. Hiao-Tsim Ma. When Yo-Yo was young, Dr. Ma set forth five principles to guide his career development: organization, concentration, memorization, constant practice, and discipline. Guided by these principles, Yo-Yo was able to achieve what most people can only dream of. For example, he developed the extraordinary ability to memorize notes. As a result, he does not have to depend on sheet music when he performs, freeing him to be creative in his performance and take the music to a higher level.[32]

As introduced before, in ancient China, if a student was lazy or did not perform in school, he would be caned by the teacher. If he did not deliver a good academic performance, he would be caned by his father at home. In today's Chinese society, although the corporal punishment of children is no longer allowed, parents are much stricter than in most American families. They still hold the core value that childhood is the best time to learn and to prepare children for their future. As a result, they expect of their children to learn more, deliver top-notch academic performance, and to strictly avoid bad influences such as drugs and violence.

As a very strict example, "Tiger Mom" Amy Chua NEVER allowed her two daughters, Sophia and Louisa, to do the following ten things:[33]

- Attend a sleepover
- Have a play date
- Be in a school play
- Complain about not being in a school play
- Watch TV or play computer games
- Choose their own extracurricular activities
- Get any grade less than an A
- Not be the #1 student in every subject except gym and drama
- Play any instrument other than the piano or violin
- Not play the piano or violin

Aside from the above, her two daughters were required to learn fluent Chinese and practice 90 minutes per day on their musical instruments. They were asked to practice their instruments even while they were on vacation in another country.

If such stringent parenting seems shocking, you cannot imagine how demanding parents in China can be. Due to extremely intense employment pressure and fierce competition to get into universities in China, most schoolchildren are required to study seven days a week, 12-16 hours per day. They have to go to school every weekday for 8 hours and follow that up with 2-4 hours of homework. In addition, they have to learn and practice English and learn at least one type of musical instrument. All students have to go to school during the weekend for extra classes, or in preparation for science, mathematics, or other types of competition. Typically, most students in China study or practice the same long hours as Sophia and Louisa did. The worst part is most Chinese students have no chance to take vacations like Sophia and Louisa did. Starting from kindergarten, they have to work hard continuously until they are admitted to college. It is worth mentioning that Korean parents also demand that their children study long hours, an average of 7.6 hours at school and many hours in cram schools after their regular classes. In order to curb such unhealthy trends, the Korean government sends inspectors to close down many night schools after 10:00 p.m.[34]

Does every parent need to become a "Tiger Mom"? Should every parent place the same demands on their children as parents in China or Korea? The answer in most cases is: Not necessarily.

In the US, the ratio of student college enrollment and high school graduates is significantly higher. In addition, the US has many more top-ranked universities that offer many enrollment opportunities for American high school graduates. The road to higher education is not as crowded as in China. Let's have an objective assessment: If it can be said the U.S. public education approach is too lenient, then by the same token the Chinese public education approach is too strict. The right balance, then, is somewhere in between. This is the approach taken by most Chinese American families in the US. Their children do not have to study the kind of long hours as the students in China, but they study significantly longer than the average American student. This is the kind of study ethic Chinese American parents typically expect from their children.

Jerry Yang, co-founder of Yahoo, recalls that when he was in school, his parents asked him to study longer than most of his classmates.

When he attended a party with his parents, they typically allowed him to play sports with friends for one hour and then do one hour of math exercises. To most American students this sounds like too much study. As Jerry said, however, it was actually less than Taiwanese students. In their case, they got to study for two hours and had to forego the one hour of play.[35]

Andrea Jung, the former CEO of Avon Cosmetics, tells a similar story. Her parents signed her up for Chinese classes every Saturday morning, piano practice every weekday afternoon, and evening musical recitals on the weekends. In this way, she developed not only skills, but also a strong work ethic that benefited her later during her career development.[36]

As the above examples illustrate, reasonably strict parenting methods can yield convincing results. As successful as they are inspired to be, many Chinese/Asian American students realize their dream through their passion for education and strong work ethic: 92.2% of 2009 high school graduates enrolled in college. Many of them went on to attend America's most prestigious universities, including Ivy League schools, Stanford University, MIT, and UC Berkeley.

In the case of the family of "Tiger Mom," Sophia and Louisa had to work much harder than average Chinese American children because their mother, Amy Chua, had set objectives for them to become top performers on the piano and violin, respectively. Both instruments require extraordinarily intensive training and practice. Moreover, the competition in these fields is extremely intense, in particular from students with Asian heritage or those from China and other Asian countries. In our neighborhood, there is a family in which both parents are in the music profession. In order to train their son to become a top violinist, they selected to home school him for many years. They believed if he went to public school he would not have enough time to practice the violin. I can easily appreciate the effort Amy, my neighbor, and their children made. However, if your children do not choose such highly competitive professions as their future careers, there is no need to be as strict as Amy in terms of demanding children so thoroughly devote themselves to learning. My wife and I do not require our children to study or practice the same long hours. Most Chinese American families I know do not set up such strict requirements either.

Being less strict about study time does not mean parents should be lenient in regard to their children's social behavior. Confucianism-influenced Chinese parents also have a distinctive approach in this area. I will elaborate on this in Chapter 7.

Being reasonably strict does not equate to not loving your children. It means being responsible for your children's future. This piece of wisdom, drawn directly from Confucianism, is widely embraced by Chinese people wherever they live.

It is important to mention that the publication of *Battle Hymn of the Tiger Mom* helped give rise to the stereotype of Chinese Americans as being too extreme, too strict in their parenting. This is not true for my family nor for most Chinese American families I know. From the example of Jerry Yang and many others, you can clearly see Chinese American parenting styles are reasonably strict while maintaining a good balance of study and play. On the one hand, they ask their children to study and participate in extracurricular activities more than the average American family because they believe in a good work ethic. Based on their cultural heritage, they believe human potential can be further tapped by those willing to make the extra effort. Very importantly, it is because they understand that current American public education fails to uphold a reasonable standard aimed at preparing their children to meet the challenge of the global competition posed by China, India, Korea, Russia, Brazil, and other rapidly growing economies. On the other hand, most Chinese American families treasure the childhood of their children. They arrange reasonable playtimes for their children. They take them on vacation to Disneyworld and other fun places. As you may notice if you visit Disneyworld or other similar family vacation destinations in the US, there is a much higher percentage of Chinese American visitors than their 1.2% national ratio would suggest. You will also see many cases of Chinese American parents holding video cameras, passionately recording every joyful moment of their children. They love their children no less than other races. They just take a balanced approach in how they manifest their affection.

In some American schools, top-performing Asian students are ridiculed for their excellent performance. Some people misperceive outstanding Asian Americans as a threat to their job opportunities. Many of them do not realize it is just such hard-working Asian Americans who contribute significantly to the success of American's high-tech companies such Intel, Microsoft, Google, and Apple. These companies generate huge export sales, profits, and dividends for the American economy and shareholders. They are the backbone of the American economy and make the U.S. competitive globally.

As introduced in Chapter 1, with increasing global competition and tremendous domestic challenges such as public and individual debt and Social Security and Medicare solvency issues, many Americans, if they want to have a good quality of life, need to change their behavior. This includes improving the work/study ethic for the younger generation. They can help themselves by learning and adopting inspiring Confucian values. Being reasonably strict with your children is one important tenet of Confucian values.

#5 Create a Virtuous Circle of Study

Why do American students, on average, lag behind European and Asian students in mathematics and science education? Why do many children, after first showing signs of a drop in academic performance, then proceed to a vicious circle of worsening academic performance before finally dropping out of school? There are many reasons, and education method is a critical one. Amazingly, the solution can be found in two educational principles laid out by Confucians 2,500 years ago—the second and third educational principles I introduced in section 5.2.

Confucianism, in its *Book of Rites,* says a good teacher is one who can keep and encourage a student's interest in learning (善教者，使人继其志). It points out that in order to maintain this interest, a teacher needs to make learning a journey that is both enjoyable and challenging. Another principle in the *Book of Rites* illustrates that one key successful teaching method is to base the progress on a student's aptitude and learned knowledge (大学之法…不凌节而施之为孙). This principle would be interpreted by Chinese people to mean teaching/learning needs to develop gradually by following its proper steps and sequence (循序渐进). It underscores the need to build a foundation of prerequisite knowledge before further progress can be made.

Seen another way, learning many subjects such as mathematics and the sciences is like building a skyscraper. In order to build a tall and stable skyscraper, the first step is to lay a solid foundation. After the foundation is laid and has passed quality inspection, the builder can begin to construct the first story, then the second story, and so on. The builder needs to make sure each step has been completed in a satisfactory manner before proceeding to the next step.

Unfortunately, either in an attempt to protect the "self-esteem" of every student or guided by the misbelief that reasonable learning requirements are to blame for denying students' opportunity for further education, many schools in the US relax their academic standards in the pursuit of higher graduation rates: They lower test standards and assign lenient grades to students who otherwise would not have passed the exams. As a result, many students who have not built a solid foundation in elementary school enter into middle school. These students in turn enter into high school with an even more unreliable foundation. And many of these students eventually enter into college. What are the consequences?

A student in middle school math class will lose interest quickly if s/he did not lay a solid math foundation in elementary school. While many classmates are progressing, such a student has a significant knowledge gap to bridge. With insufficient elementary school math knowledge, s/he cannot comprehend what the middle school teacher is teaching. Consequently, s/he becomes frustrated with learning math and loses interest. Learning becomes a burden to this student rather than enjoyable as it should be. This creates a vicious circle of learning. If the parents or teacher do not intervene, the chances of the student learning math well become minimal. Without a sufficient foundation in math, learning science and engineering will become even more difficult down the road. American schools are filled with such stories. Sadly, the student fails, not because s/he lacks the ability to learn, but because proper methods of learning were not applied and timely help from his/her parents was not there. As a result of such failure, according to a 2010 study by UCLA's Higher Education Research Institute, "only 36% of white, 21% of African Americans, and 22% of Hispanic undergraduate students in the science, technology, engineering and math majors finished their bachelor's degrees within five years of initial enrollment."[37] The simple truth here is that the elementary, middle, and high schools did not lay a foundation of science and math sufficient for a college education.

Confucianism-influenced Chinese families fully understand this essential of learning: If you do not truly understand it or are not good at it, you will not enjoy learning it even if you are given a good grade. They use three very effective approaches to create a virtuous circle of learning. As you will notice, all three approaches are aimed at creating a solid foundation of knowledge and a leading position for your children's learning.

The first is to lay a good foundation for study at an early age. A lot of Chinese families start pre-school learning for their kids, teaching them Chinese poems, English letters, simple words, and numbers. The purpose is to cultivate interest in children to learn and be good at it. If they are good at learning, they will continue to approach it with strong self-motivation.

The second is to implement a high standard. In order to make sure children lay a solid academic foundation, most Chinese families expect their children to get As and finish every class with a sufficient understanding of the subject. This is essential to ensure that the children really learn the subject and are prepared to move to the next grade level. Equally important, being an all-A student creates a sense of pride and motivation for children to learn more. It is very important to prevent children from dropping to a mediocre level in which they risk losing the motivation to become excellent.

The third is to closely monitor the child and provide help as soon as his/her academic performance starts to drop. This can happen for an array of reasons, including social distractions or encountering a difficult academic subject. If the parents do not get to the heart of the problem on time, the child may enter a vicious circle: failure to understand the subject => difficulty in learning more => loss of confidence and interest in the subject. At this critical juncture, the parents need to step in and provide the necessary help, including tutoring, so the child can get back on track with his/her learning. Many Chinese families handle learning setbacks with their children using just such an approach. With such timely intervention and assistance, their children can maintain good momentum in their learning.

In *Battle Hymn of the Tiger Mom*, Amy Chua tells a good story. "Once, Sophia [Amy's daughter] came in second on a multiplication speed test, which her fifth-grade teacher administered every Friday. She lost to a Korean boy named Yoon-seok. Over the next week, I made Sophia do twenty practice tests (of 100 problems each) every night, with me clocking her with a stopwatch. After that, she came in first every time."[38] Many American parents may not value the merit of winning first place for Sophia. However, a responsible parent should take the same action Amy did if their child is having difficulty learning or understanding a subject. It is very important to continuously enable them to be good at the subject and maintain their interest in learning it.

Coincidently, I did a similar exercise with my daughter Selena. I bought a few math speed exercise books and put them to use when Selena started to learn multiplication and division and the school exercises were proving inadequate for her. With our intensive training, she learned multiplication and division sufficiently and reached a good level of proficiency. I know many Chinese parents would do the same thing when faced with a similar situation because it is the most effective way to usher a child into the virtuous circle of learning.

Once parents succeed in helping their children toward a virtuous circle of learning, it creates a win-win-win situation for the children, the parents, and the teacher: Children are in their learning comfort zone, they are self-motivated to learn more, and they have a sense of pride about learning. Parents do not have to tutor their children intensively, and the teacher will have another happy student willing to learn. Is this not the situation many parents dream of?

5.4 How to Combine the Strengths of the American and Confucian Education Approaches

After being exposed to the many strengths of the Confucian style of education, readers may ask: Does this mean the Western education approach is not as good as the Asian approach?

Clearly this is neither the author's opinion nor his intent. As the main engine of modern civilization, Western society has generated a host of world-class approaches to science, learning, and education. Based on my experience living and studying in two countries across two distinctive cultures, I see a big advantage in combining the strengths of both the American and Chinese education approaches. This strategy will surely improve educational effectiveness and enable your children to realize a better life in the years to come.

As I have already described some of the strengths of the Confucian education approach, in the pages that follow I'd like to emphasize a few valuable strengths of the American/Western education approach that readers should continue to practice:

1. Develop multidimensional skills, not just knowledge learning

Modern Western/American education practices emphasize comprehensive skill development, including the teaching of knowledge, communication, leadership, personal skills, volunteering, and other ethical values. In comparison, traditional Chinese teaching primarily emphasizes knowledge learning and moral development. In American schools, students are presented with various formats of learning: classroom lecture, class discussion and participation, presentation, various school projects and field trips. Today, scholars all over the world, including Chinese scholars, agree that multidimensional skill development for students is the right education approach for students.

2. Emphasize independent thinking, instead of just memorizing knowledge

As I wrote earlier, when Confucius established his theories, he emphasized the importance of thinking (思) in the process of learning

(学). He said: "Learning without thinking leads to confusion; thinking without learning leads to failure (学而不思则罔，思而不学则殆)." Clearly he means to strike a good balance between learning the existing knowledge and thinking, digesting of the knowledge. Mencius goes one step further: "If you believe all the things in the book "Shang", it is worse than not reading the book (尽信书，则不如无书)."[39] It was a clear endorsement of healthy skepticism. However, after Confucianism became a dominant socio-political value system in China, Chinese teachers tended to emphasize the knowledge learning part of education, not the independent thinking and skepticism part. It was the Western education practice that widely promoted independent thinking and reasonable skepticism and incorporated them as daily practices in modern education. They have been proven to be valuable approaches to improving the learning and training process. They greatly enhance students' ability to digest knowledge and develop knowledge for themselves. It is essential to encourage children/students to think independently while exercising healthy skepticism during the learning process.

3. Encourage individual creativity and outside-the-box thinking

In any single ideology-driven society, teaching runs the risk of deteriorating into preaching—learning only one school of knowledge blindly. This stifles creativity and innovation. Modern Western education practice encourages individual creativity and outside-the-box thinking. This education approach has helped to release an enormous amount of human wisdom/creativity, which in turn has helped to create our modern society. Human innovation has seen more developments in the last two centuries than in all the centuries preceding them combined. Today, individual creativity and outside-the-box thinking have become critical skills for people both young and mature.

4. Connect learning to real-world needs in the workplace and/or daily life

This is another strength of the American education approach. From elementary school to college, the teachers assign a lot of real-world projects for the student to do. This approach effectively connects classroom learning to real-world needs. It trains students to apply knowledge learned to the real world and become effective problem solvers in the future.

Many of you may not know that, in the last three decades, Chinese schools have gradually learned and adopted these strengths of the Western/American education approach. At the same time, they still uphold many of the advantages of the Confucian education approach. This explains why more and more Chinese students are excelling in various international competitions and Shanghai students were ranked #1 in the *OECD Programme for International Student Assessment (PISA)* student assessment report of 2009. When students in China, Korea, Japan, and Singapore have the benefit of combining the strengths of both Confucianism and Western education approaches, they yield good results and become increasingly competitive in the global market.

That said, there are a few challenges we need to deal with when combining the strengths of the two systems.

The first is in the area of setting up student objectives. They need to be aimed at developing multidimensional skills. High academic performance is essential for children to learn fundamental knowledge and develop other skills. However, it must expand into social skills, such as communication, leadership, team working and other areas.

The second is addressing the balance between children's playtime, sports time, and extra study time. As we introduced earlier, students in China are overwhelmed by all-day study and other academic activities. On the other hand, American students spend much of their after-school hours in recreation or doing sports. What is the right balance? To meet future career challenges, I recommend the following for school-age children:

- Spend enough time learning the school curriculum and reach preferably the A-grade level.
- Make an extra effort to learn mathematics, science, languages, and other social sciences to expand or strengthen children's

knowledge base. This can be achieved through participation in various school clubs and/or competitions.

- Master at least one additional language. It is a proven way to expand career opportunities.
- Participate in sports or outdoor activities on a weekly basis.
- Reasonable daily playtime as well as on the weekends.
- If the children can handle the school curriculum with ease, musical instruments and other types of arts can be added.

The precise ratio can vary depending on the children's intelligence level, academic performance, interests, and other factors. It is important to incorporate a good combination of learning and outdoor activities. One effective approach parents can take is to develop a schedule for children's after-school activities. The schedule should outline time slots for study, sports, play, foreign language, and music. In this way, it is easier to maintain a good balance between children's study time and playtime.

Parents also should take advantage of modern technologies, encouraging children to watch a prescribed amount of TV programs that have both educational and entertainment value. It is a one-stone-two-birds approach that provides both recreation and knowledge for children. Channels with worthwhile programming include: National Geographic, History Channel, Discovery Channel, Science Channel, and Animal Planet.

My wife and I have been taking this balanced approach in parenting our own children, Hubert and Selena. First, we make sure they build a solid academic foundation. Both of them have been straight-A students from elementary school to middle school. Second, we encourage them to participate in sports and other extracurricular activities. Hubert takes part in soccer, kung fu, track, swimming, and other sports—one at a time. He used to play piano and is learning guitar now. Selena has been a dancer and orchestra violinist. Third, we encourage them to develop social skills, such as leadership, speech, and debate. In addition, both of them are learning Chinese, one of the most important languages for the twenty-first century. That is a typical weekday's agenda for them.

On the weekends, like most American parents, we go to soccer games, watch TV, and play Mahjong or cards with them. The children go to parties and attend other recreational activities, having fun with their friends. Unlike "Tiger Mom," we allow Selena to attend sleepovers, but only with trusted friends. We have taken them on vacation to many places and countries, and all in all we want them to have a wonderful childhood.

This combined Confucian-Western parenting approach has yielded great results. In the recently finished school year, Hubert received the prestigious 4-D Award for eighth grade, and Selena received the prestigious Navigator Award for seventh grade from Discovery Middle School in Orlando, an A-rated school. Both awards are given to the top girl and the top boy in the entire grade based on all-around achievement. That school year, Hubert also won the Junior National Beta Convention Science Competition Championship, while Selena was elected president of her school's Beta Club and won third place in the State Junior Beta Convention Speech Competition. With such extraordinary accomplishments, they have developed a true sense of self-esteem and enjoy learning. As caring and responsible parents, we have experienced the twofold joy of our kids enjoying their childhood while taking great pride in every one of their accomplishments in learning skills for their future.

Based on our real-life experience, I recommend a balanced approach to education that focuses on multidimensional skill development with standards stricter than the average level of American school age children but more lenient than the average level of students in China. I strongly believe an approach that combines the strengths of both the Chinese and American education systems can lead to much better results than an approach that uses just one of them.

Chapter 6.

THIRD VALUE: *JIE-JIAN* (节俭)

"Saving for a Better Life"—Confucian Value of Managing Money Conservatively and Wisely

6.1 IMPORTANCE OF MONEY MANAGEMENT IN TODAY'S AMERICA

Most Americans did not realize how bad money management was in this country until the financial crisis that started in 2008. According to U.S. statistics, the total amount of consumer debt in the United States stands at nearly $2.4 trillion. Based on 2010 Census data, that works out to nearly $7,800 of debt for every man, woman, and child in the US. With the flood of consumer credit, many Americans indulge in irresponsible consumption: They live beyond their means. According to the Federal Reserve Bank, 40 percent of households spend more than they earn.[1]

On the savings side, the U.S. savings rate has been declining since the 1980s. In the late 1970s and early 1980s, Americans had a savings rate of between 10% and 14.9% of their personal income. In the early 1980s, the American credit revolution made credit widely available to American consumers. Ever since then, Americans have changed their behavior, and the personal savings rate dropped to 5% or less.[2] According to a Wells Fargo Retirement Survey in 2011, "A majority of middle class Americans (53%) say they 'need to significantly cut back on spending today to save for retirement.' Americans have saved, on average, only 7% of their desired retirement nest egg—a median of $25,000 in retirement savings vs. a median retirement goal of $350,000. Three in ten people (29%) in their 60s have saved less than $25,000 for retirement, possibly indicating they will rely heavily on Social Security."[3]

As a comparison, the savings rate in China is about 25%, which means on average the Chinese save one fourth of their incomes.[4] By the end of 2009, Chinese consumers had a savings balance of about US$4 trillion, equal to $3,088 per capita.[5] To most Americans this might not seem like a significantly high number. However, the GDP in China is only $3,011 per capita. By the same ratio, U.S. personal savings per capita should be about $48,000 because U.S. GDP per capita in 2009 was about $47,000.

In addition to the unsustainable behavior of living beyond their means, many Americans suffer from a lack of money management skills. During the housing market boom, greedy mortgage lenders at Countrywide were able to issue 49% of its mortgages as adjustable rate mortgages, which one by one became time bombs that eventually exploded, forcing many of these borrowers into foreclosure.[6] Similarly, many people used high interest rate credit cards without constraints, which drove them into personal bankruptcy. These are all signs of an inability to manage money and to fend off greedy lenders.

Living beyond their means, and having no sufficient savings as a buffer, many Americans depend on the very next paycheck to survive. In 2009 alone, about 1.3 million people filed for bankruptcy and 2.8 million lost their homes as a result of foreclosure, largely due to the impact of the financial crisis and partly due to poor money management.[7,8] The economic prospects of many American individuals are bleak at best.

Unfortunately, financial reliance on the government is worsening. The US accumulated over $16 trillion in government debt by 2012. This is likely to lead to a reduction of benefits and/or delay in payment of Social Security and Medicare. What does this mean to most Americans? You cannot count on receiving the full benefits of Social Security and Medicare. You have to take a better approach to managing your money.

6.2 CONFUCIAN VALUE OF *JIE-JIAN* (节俭): SAVING FOR A BETTER LIFE

Saving, called *jie-jian* (节俭) in Chinese, is a core Confucian value. When Confucius handled his first administrative jobs, managing a warehouse and dairy farm, he was able to increase wealth and built a reputation for effectiveness. When the duke of the state of Qi asked Confucius to define the essence of managing a nation, Confucius answered: Saving.[9] In the *Book of Rites*, the concept of "**size your spending based on your income** (量入而出)" was set down more than 2,500 years ago.[10] Very likely, it is one of the earliest recorded money management rules in human history. In today's language, it says: Do not live beyond your means!

In addition to this basic rule, Confucius laid out a cornerstone of money management: "The main principle of creating wealth is: There should be more people in producing wealth than those in spending. Those who produce wealth should work fast and those who spend should use the money slowly. In this way, wealth will be created sufficiently and sustainably (生财有大道，生之者众，食之者寡，为之者疾，用之者舒，则财恒足矣。)."[11] This principle illustrates three key aspects of wealth management:

1. *The need to produce wealth/income*
2. *The need to control spending, to save*
3. *The need to have more/faster income creation than spending*

This comprises the golden rule of wealth management. Throughout human history, one pattern has emerged: Those who follow this principle have managed their wealth well. They create financial security for their families. On the other hand, those who fail to follow this principle are likely get into financial trouble.

Confucianism promotes saving as its core value of money management and, equally important, as a core ethical value. In the Confucian value system, overspending and wasting are considered unethical behaviors. The failing dynasties in the Chinese history were usually associated with too much spending and too much taxation, which demoralized the citizens and weakened the nation. In contrast, wise emperors were always associated with saving and other good behaviors. A famous poet of the Tang Dynasty, Li Shang Yin (李商隐~812–858), wrote: "If we look at all previous eras of the nation and every family, success is always associated with saving and being broke always caused by the pursuit of lavishness (历览前贤国与家，成由勤俭破由奢。)."[12]

Another famous poet of the Tang Dynasty, Li Sheng (李绅, 772–846), in his famous poem "Sympathy to Farmers," wrote: "The farmer plants the rice seedlings during a hot noon time; His sweat drops down into the soil together with the rice seedlings; When you eat the rice from the bowl, do you know that each piece of rice is produced with hard work (锄禾日当午，汗滴禾下土; 谁知盘中餐，粒粒皆辛苦？)."[13] After it was written, this touching poem was selected as one of 300 Tang poems that every Chinese child is asked to memorize. It spread to every Chinese family and was cited most often by parents to teach children the virtue of being thrifty and saving. In ancient China, according to Confucian ethics, whether poor or rich, people are not supposed to waste food. Always finishing the last piece of rice in your bowl is a basic ethical requirement for Confucianism-influenced families.

Influenced by Confucianism as well as popular teaching such as "Sympathy to Farmers," the concepts of saving, thrift, and responsible money management have become rooted in almost every Chinese family. It has become embedded in Chinese culture and accompanies every Chinese everywhere s/he goes. The Chinese success—in Southeast Asia, in the US—all has something to do with such values. Today, with improvements in the standard of living, the Chinese people are not as thrifty as they once were, when they saved every penny. However, the majority of Chinese still hold a few core money management approaches that enable them to succeed, whether they live in China or abroad. ***This is the third Chinese secret for success: managing money conservatively and wisely.*** I will introduce these core money management approaches one by one in the following section.

6.3 HOW CHINESE FAMILIES UTILIZE *JIE-JIAN* (节俭) TO SAVE AND USE THEIR MONEY WISELY

What key approaches do Confucianism-influenced Chinese families use to manage their money? How are they different from those practiced by average Americans? Based on my bicultural life experience, and my observation of many Chinese families in China and in the US, I believe the following distinctive approaches are worth elaborating on.

#1 Be Thrifty; Do Not Waste

In Chinese, the most popular four-character idiom on managing family wealth is called *qin-jian-chi-jia* (勤俭持家), which means you should work hard and be thrifty to manage family wealth. This idiom is used by almost every family in China. If one spouse buys an item the family can't afford, the other spouse may use this idiom to remind him/her that they need to be thrifty. When the children grow up, parents always use this idiom to teach them to practice thrifty habits. As a norm of money management this concept has thoroughly infiltrated Chinese society.

In both the US and China consumers tend to shop for less. They try to get good deals and buy in bulk in order to save money. These behaviors clearly are essential elements of thrift.

In comparison with American consumers, the Chinese stress another important aspect of thrift: Do not waste. It first is reflected in the usage of energy, water, food, and other consumables. As mentioned earlier, Chinese are taught to value even a single piece of rice because they know, deep in their heart, that it takes hard work to produce anything. Although modern advances have improved production technology in many areas, most Chinese families still have relatives living in poor Chinese villages and less advanced regions. It becomes morally unconscionable if they waste resources while their relatives still struggle in underprivileged existences. As a result, they uphold a strong moral sense of "do not waste." Most Chinese families are very conscious in terms of saving energy. They turn off lights when they leave the room. In hot summers, they do not set the thermostat too low because they know that setting it a couple of degrees higher will use far less energy. For the same reason, in the winter, they do not set the thermostat too high. In terms of food and other disposables, they try not to buy more than they need, and throw away as little as possible.

The second aspect of "do not waste" is reflected in their buying decisions. In most Chinese families, before any purchase, the question is posed: "Do I need this? Do we already have something I can use instead?" This is another area with a huge potential for saving. By eliminating unnecessary purchases, a family can stop the waste and save money for other more important things, such as retirement and the children's education. In American society, many consumers have been misled by the slogan: "The more you buy, the more you save." This slogan is simply part of a marketing campaign designed to encourage the overbuying and overuse of products, but not a good guide for your buying decisions. Partially influenced by such slogans, some American consumers have become shopaholics, routinely buying unnecessary goods that get stored in closets or garages and see little or no use. You will rarely find this kind of waste in Chinese American families.

The third aspect of "do not waste" is reflected in the decision to replace reliable goods, such as cars, furniture, televisions, and appliances. Influenced by Confucianism, most Chinese families still hold the view that if it functions and still provides its intended purpose, it does not need replacing. Cars, furniture, televisions, and appliances entail high-dollar purchases. The less frequently you replace them, the more you will save in the long run.

#2 Make Value-Based Purchases

Being thrifty is a key feature of Confucian money management. Does it mean that you always buy cheap stuff and have a poor standard of living? Twenty-five hundred years ago, Confucius said, "[Although] lavishness runs the risk of not being modest, thrift may lead to being meager (奢则不孙，俭则固)." Although Confucius values thrift over lavishness (与其不孙也，宁固), he clearly recognizes the shortcoming of being *too* thrifty.[14]

Contrary to stereotype, most Chinese American families are not always thrifty. Most of them live in nice neighborhoods in a nice house typically in good school districts, drive name-brand cars such as Honda and Toyota, and have name-brand televisions, computers, and other consumer products. At popular family vacation destinations such as Disneyworld and Seaworld you will find the percentage of Chinese visitors is significantly higher than their percentage in the American population, indicating they are not focused solely on saving—they also spend time and money enjoying life!

What are their secrets? The first is making value-based purchases. For example, if a Honda vehicle can give you better gas mileage, three more years of life, less trouble in repairs, and a higher resale value than a Hyundai, most Chinese will buy the Honda. In reaching this decision, they consider not only the initial purchase price, but also additional monetary costs such as maintenance, repair costs, and resale value. In addition, non-monetary considerations such as reliability and social image are also taken into account.

Another example of a value-based purchase pertains to electronics. These types of products reflect a steep drop in price between new products that have just been made available and market-tested products that have been available for some time. Take for example the camcorder. When it was first introduced each unit cost thousands of dollars. Just a few years later, that price had dropped to hundreds of dollars. When an electronics manufacturer introduces new product features, such as high definition TV, there are high R&D (research and development) costs to be recouped. As a result, the initial cost is significantly higher. On top of that, pricing strategists typically use a "skim" strategy in pricing such products. Basically, they add a much higher profit margin to newly introduced products because early adopters typically are willing to pay more. Armed with this knowledge, how should you approach the purchase of new electronics? Always buy just-released products and pay the premium or wait a few months after the price has dropped significantly? For most Americans with a limited income, it is not worthwhile to pay the premium because waiting a few months will not significantly impact your pleasure of consumption. This is the approach most Chinese Americans take: Make purchases based on the product value, not on fashion.

In addition to making value-based purchases, Chinese have an untold secret: spending money differently on those goods you will possess and those things you will use temporarily. Although the doctrine of communism dominated China from 1949 to 1979, most Chinese still embody the core values: They care about their family and themselves the most. For things they do not possess, just use temporarily, they are not willing to spend a lot of money. For goods they will possess, they are willing to pay more, buy name-brand products. A good example is staying in a hotel vs. buying a house. A Chinese family will pay a premium to buy a nice house because it is something they will own. However, the same Chinese family will not spend money on unnecessarily extravagant hotel accommodations when they travel. The reason is that the money goes to someone else. The same logic applies to buying a car vs. renting a car. For the same reason, most Chinese American families do not go out to eat as often as Americans of the same income level. Spending less on the goods you do not possess is clearly a desirable approach when you do not have a high income. You need to build your assets first.

#3 Save, Always Keep Some Surplus (节约，留有富余)

Saving, always keeping some surplus, is the most distinctive money management approach adopted by almost every Chinese family. This is the most traditional and simplest way used by most Chinese families to build their assets.

In chapter 6.2, I introduced the principle of Confucian money management: Spending should be less than income generation. This means that you should always have savings, have some surplus. Over the last 2,500 years, this concept has taken root in every Chinese family.

Between January and February of each year, Chinese people celebrate their most important holiday, the Chinese New Year, which is determined by the lunar calendar. All family members usually come together to celebrate the New Year, in particular attending dinner on New Year's Eve. They prepare ten more delicious dishes for the dinner of the year. Among them, there is always fish. Westerners unacquainted with Chinese culture do not understand the importance of having fish on the New Year's dinner table. This is not because fish is good for heart health, nutrition, or taste reasons. It is because of a symbolic reason. Because the pronunciation of fish "Yu" is the same as the pronunciation of "surplus" in Chinese, also called "Yu," having a fish dish on the New Year's Eve dinner table signifies the family will have a surplus for the coming year (年年有余/鱼). The fish on New Year's Eve dinner sends a powerful message to the family, reminding every family member to save, to have some surplus for the family each year. From this simple example you can see that the Confucian concept of "saving, having surplus" is deeply rooted and widely spread in Chinese culture. It explains why Chinese people have on average a savings rate of 25%.

Chinese people all over the world keep this valuable tradition. They know that, by having some savings, they can pursue better lives than those who do not save. They put themselves in the proactive mode of money management, an essential step in creating financial security. When the financial crisis hit the U.S. real estate market and property prices plummeted, many Chinese Americans moved quickly to take advantage of this market opportunity. They either bought a larger house to live in or bought houses as investment properties. Many Chinese Americans could do this not because they were very rich, but because they had savings, and a very good credit history.

With some savings at hand, you are in much better shape to deal with life's unexpected mishaps. Everybody encounters them from time to time. A family member may become injured or sick. Someone may lose a job, in particular during an economic downturn. I personally knew a few Chinese who lost their jobs during the financial crisis. However, because they had savings, they managed to survive for a year or longer without having to sell their house or other properties.

Equally important, saving money will provide a reserve for other major family spending in the future. Once the children are grown, there will be the cost of a college education. After you retire, you will need money to supplement social security. When your children get married, you may want to help pay for the wedding. The list goes on. But the key requirement is the same: Have some savings. Do not use up everything you earn!

By contrast, spending everything you earn will put your money management into a reactive mode. If you depend on your next paycheck to survive, you will not have the financial buffer to handle any mishaps you may encounter. You will go into debt immediately if you lose your job or have a major family mishap. If the situation persists or deteriorates, you can end up losing your house and/or your personal property—you may even have to file for personal bankruptcy. Over the last three years, I have heard about and observed too many such unfortunate stories in the US.

How can you prevent this from happening to your family? You need to take an active approach to money management: Establish a monthly and annual family budget that includes contingency spending and savings. Following is a good approach to establishing a family budget:

- *First, calculate your household income.* You need to start with the total monthly household income earned by you and your spouse. This is the total maximum amount you can spend.
- *Second, calculate your average monthly spending.* This includes major items, rent/mortgage, fuel, insurance, groceries, medical payments, etc. When you calculate spending, you need to take into account seasonal effects. For example, higher air conditioning costs in the summer and higher heating costs in the winter. Summarize the total average monthly spending.

- ***Third, decide on a contingency/saving rate.*** Look ahead at the major purchases you will need to make in the near future, such as a car, a set of furniture, or a vacation. Devote enough savings to cover that. On the top of that, you need to leave money for retirement or emergency funds in case of an unexpected mishap. The savings rate should be based on your stage of life and economic conditions. When you are in your twenties and early thirties, your salary is not very high. It is generally at this time that you start a family, buy a house, and raise your children. It is okay for you to have a lower savings rate. But you should try your best to have some savings, let's say at least 10% of your income. When you reach middle age and your income is higher, you need to increase the savings rate to at least 20% to prepare for your retirement and maybe your children's education. There are many books about retirement planning that you can use as reference. In any case, you need to save money both for the future and for contingencies. After you arrive at your savings rate, apply it to your monthly income. This will be the monthly savings you want to achieve.
- ***Fourth, combine your total monthly spending and savings.*** This becomes your monthly budget.
- ***Fifth, compare your monthly income and budget and make adjustments, if needed.*** If your average monthly budget is greater than your monthly income, you need to cut spending as feasibly as possible. If it is still not enough, you will have to adjust your savings rate downward. Nevertheless, maintaining a reasonable savings rate of 10-20% of your income is key.
- ***Sixth, make annual adjustments.*** You may receive a year-end bonus that varies in amount each year. Similarly, what you require for Christmas shopping may vary each year depending on the purchases you need to make. This is why you need to make an annual adjustment before you go out Christmas shopping. The bonus can be used to contribute to contingency savings. However, do not depend for all of your savings on your annual bonus unless it is a consistent amount you can depend

on every year. At the end of the year, if there is a shortfall in your income, you need to reduce Christmas spending accordingly in order to avoid overspending. In essence, try to achieve at least 15% savings as a good money management approach.

Establishing a budget that includes savings and contingency is a smart and essential way to manage your money. If you do it the other way around, first spend and then save what's left, you will have a much greater tendency to spend all you earn and have nothing left for savings.

#4 Do Not Borrow, Unless It's Absolutely Necessary and at a Very Low Interest Rate

Most American families' financial troubles have something to do with debt and borrowing. Foreclosure happens when a property owner is unable or unwilling to make payments on his/her mortgage debt. Personal bankruptcy is the result of a borrower having an inability to pay off his/her outstanding debt.

Objectively speaking, borrowing and financing form a necessary lubricant for the gears of the modern economy. They also provide huge benefits to consumers. With mortgage lending, people can buy their dream house when they are still young. They do not have to wait twenty years until they've saved enough money to buy a house. For needy students, the student loan program enables them to go to college and repay the debt after they get a job. Car loans likewise help consumers to spread a huge purchase over 36-60 monthly payments that are easier to handle.

However, consumer lending in the US is a highly troubled area of finance that has been abused by greedy lenders and irresponsible/ignorant borrowers alike. Bankers "innovate" all kinds of ways to entice consumers to borrow, sending out credit cards and offering rebates and discounts to potential borrowers. Mortgage lenders launch aggressive marketing campaign, offering many options to attract those in the market to purchase or refinance a home. Some are adjustable rate mortgages or other similarly risky mortgages. I personally saw many refinance offers that actually cost you more money even though the lender claimed a lower monthly payment: They quietly extended the payment terms. Some title loan companies give you a very high interest loan with one very high-risk condition: They use your car as collateral. Without a full understanding of the financial consequences, many borrowers took the loans, unknowingly stepping into troubled water. What are the results? In 2009 alone, about 1.3 million people filed for personal bankruptcy and 2.8 million lost their homes as a result of foreclosure. Tens of thousands of others lost their cars.

Unfortunately, with a poor understanding of mathematics, a large number of Americans fail to appreciate the true cost of borrowing. The following table serves as an illustration. Assume that you buy something for $1,000 and put it on a credit card. You keep the balance at $1,000, putting each payment toward the interest (In this example, we assume the borrower makes a minimum payment of 2% and buys a very small amount of goods, keeping the credit card balance at $1000). If you are extremely lucky, you get a 4.9% interest rate, which means that over five years you will pay $245 in interest, which is 24.5% more than the amount you borrowed. That is a best-case scenario. More typically you will get an interest rate of about 14.9%, which means that over the same five years you will pay $495 in interest, almost 50% more than the amount you originally borrowed. In a worst-case scenario, such as the 59.9% interest rate charged by First Premier Bank until February 2011,[15] you will pay $2,995 in interest over five years, about three times the amount you borrowed.

Table 2. Financial Cost of Borrowing Over Five Years

Interest Rate	4.9%	9.9%	14.9%	19.9%	29.9%	59.9%
Annual Interest Payment	$49	$99	$149	$199	$299	$599
5 Year Interest Payment	$245	$495	$745	$995	$1,495	$2,995
5 Year Interest Payment As Percentage of Principle	24.5%	49.5%	74.5%	99.5%	149.5%	299.5%

After seeing these numbers, most readers start to realize something: As soon as you take out a loan or get into credit-card debt, you start working partly for the bank. The higher the interest rate, the higher the percentage of the money you earn that goes to the bank. If you have a sizable amount of debt, say a few thousand dollars, with a double-digit interest rate (10% or higher), the amount of interest you pay to the bank/lender becomes too high for the average family to handle because the debt will grow exponentially in a very short time. If you lack the resolve to pay it off or make a settlement, very soon the debt will grow to consume the earnings from all your hard work. You will become a monetary slave of the bank or lender. Do you know how much Wall Street distributes in bonuses? In 2009, the bonus allowance for the six largest banks was $150 billion.[16] On average, Wall Street employees in New York City received a bonus of $123,850 per person, more than twice the U.S. median household income.[17] How do Wall Street firms manage to earn so much money? A large percentage comes from the hundreds of thousands of unwise borrowers who do not realize they have been hard at work not so much for their own families as for Wall Street executives.

"Borrowing" and "debt" are bad words in Confucianism-influenced cultures. People in these cultures understand they have a limited income that is best devoted to their families. They are extremely stingy in terms of giving away money to the bankers. Moreover, they are afraid of being overwhelmed by debt, which they understand can destroy their lives. As a general rule, most Chinese depend on their savings to make purchases. Although living in the US, a country where financing is widely available, most Chinese Americans still live very conservatively. When it comes to borrowing they follow a few key rules:

1. Avoid any type of predatory financing that carries with it a very high interest rate (>10%), such as title loans.
2. Never leave a recurring balance on your credit card. Always pay it off when you make your monthly payment.
3. If necessary, take out a low interest rate car loan, 7% or below. Whenever you have extra money, accelerate the payment; pay it off as soon as possible.
4. Take out a low fixed rate mortgage for your house. The reason for this is because people can rarely pay cash for such a large purchase. Another reason is because the interest payment on

a mortgage is tax deductable. However, when taking out a mortgage, never choose an adjustable rate mortgage. Always choose a fixed rate mortgage. Also, if possible pay 20% down in order to avoid the need to purchase mortgage insurance.

5. Try to save for your children's college education; try to make it so they don't have to take out student loans.

6. Do not take out any other type of interest-bearing loan unless it is for a major emergency.

These money management values can be traced back to Confucius and other Chinese ancestors. It has been reinforced through formal or informal education from one generation to the next. Today, it forms a strong shield, preventing most Chinese families from falling prey to greedy bankers and predatory lenders.

If you encounter some type of family emergency, or are in a pursuit of a good cause, however, you may have no choice but to borrow. The wise move here is to pay off the debt as soon as possible and in the right sequence. In 1994, I was admitted to the Master of International Business Studies program of the University of South Carolina, then ranked as the #1 international MBA by US News and World Report. With my GMAT score and work experience, I was able to obtain a tuition waiver. However, I had to pay a one-time contribution fee of $8,100 plus stipend. Because my salary in China was only a few hundred dollars per year, I did not have sufficient savings to pay the fee. Based on good job prospects for graduates from the international MBA program at the University of South Carolina, I was determined to pursue the degree using the only financing at my disposal: credit cards (As a foreign student at that time, I was not eligible to take out a student loan). Constrained by low credit limits, I had to use four or five credit cards to make various payments. When I received my MBA and got a job two years later, I had accumulated about $10,000 in credit card debt, with interest rates ranging from 12.99% to 19.99%. After my wife and I settled down in a one-bedroom apartment in Orlando, Florida, we immediately took action to pay off the credit card debt. We made a plan: Pay off the card with the highest interest first because the accumulation of interest was adding to my debt rapidly. We controlled our spending, put aside what we could, and used no cost convenience checks from First USA bank to make the payments. One by one, we paid off all the credit cards within a year. Ever since then, we always pay off our credit card balances when we make monthly payments.

#5 Strive to Generate More Money

As mentioned in section 6.2, the Confucianism concept of money management emphasizes not only the saving side, but also the importance of generating more money. The principle is very straightforward: If you do not save your money, you will have nothing left for future use; If you do not increase your income, the amount you can save is limited.

There are many ways to generate money, but only two of them are realistic and dependable. The first is through working. The second is through investment. Let's start with the first approach:

1. Generate more money through working

Working is the most reliable to generate more money. This can be achieved in two ways: 1) working more hours, or 2) increasing your hourly earnings. Some people rely on the first approach, working long hours or taking multiple jobs. Without question this will bring more income to the family. One more hour of working leads to one more hour of pay. Many Chinese immigrants in the nineteenth century took this approach. These men worked long hours in building the American railways and doing other labor-intensive jobs. The women worked long hours in a laundry or took multiple housekeeping jobs. Nevertheless, this approach has an obvious shortcoming: Every person has only 24 hours per day. The more hours you work, the fewer hours you have left to spend resting, taking care of your family, and enjoying some recreation. Nevertheless, this is still a viable approach for those who are in no position to increase their hourly income.

Increasing your hourly earnings is clearly the preferred approach. This approach increases your income but does not need to compromise your time. It typically happens when you increase your professional experience. When you are at the entry level of a job, your salary is lowest.

As you develop more experience and job skills, you are promoted, and eventually you reach the senior level. Your salary increases accordingly. If you demonstrate managerial ability, you may be promoted to manager, which usually leads to better pay. This is typically how employees are promoted in a corporate environment. However, this is not always the case for the following reasons:

a) In some professions, the room for upward mobility is limited. For example, in the grocery business, the skill set of a more experienced retail clerk is not significantly higher than that of an entry-level clerk. You should not expect a significant increase in salary after you gain a few years of experience as a sales clerk. The same is true for many restaurant workers. In such professions, it is unlikely that you can earn a six-figure salary, unless you are promoted to a high level managerial position. In contrast, a job in an engineering firm will have more upward mobility because the relative increase in skill set at the senior level will generate more value for the company, which in turn carries with it a proportionate increase in salary.

b) Securing a job in a profession with upward mobility often requires a college degree. As in the above example of an engineering firm, professional jobs ask for a college degree as part of their minimum requirements. If you do not have a college degree, you have to stay in a non-professional job, in which the upward mobility (and commensurate salary increase) will be limited.

c) Salary increases in some professions require certification or recertification. For example, being qualified as a real estate agent entails passing exams in order to earn certification. If you have an accounting degree from an accredited college, you may get a reasonable job. But a certified public accountant (CPA) certification will advance your career and salary to another level. This kind of certification typically calls for periodic recertification.

With some basic understanding of the job market, you should evaluate: Am I in a profession that can take me to the income level I want? If not, what kind of effort do I need to make in order to enter such a profession?

Confucianism-influenced families frequently ask the above questions and make a conscious effort to pursue higher income opportunities. As the first step, they pursue a good college education from a reputable university. Throughout their career development, they acquire and maintain any necessary professional certification. For example, a large percentage of Chinese Americans who have an accounting degree will go on to become CPAs. Many Chinese go on to pursue a graduate degree because it brings with it the potential of an even higher income. This is why Chinese Americans have achieved one of the highest levels of educational attainment: over 50% received a college degree or higher education. With good education as a foundation, they aggressively pursue career opportunities that bring higher income and other benefits.

2. Generate more money through investment

Investment is another common way to generate more money. After accumulating sufficient savings, the right choice is to invest, let the money generate more money. The reason is very simple: The highest interest rate likely to accompany a savings account is typically the lowest among all investment options. The higher the return, the more money you can generate.

Chinese people have a long history of investing. In ancient times, land was the main source of agriculture income so it was the focus of Chinese investment. When a family accumulated enough savings, they bought land for farming, or even for leasing to tenant farmers. After the development of industry and commerce, many Chinese people expanded their investment to these areas. The economic successes of ethnic Chinese in Southeast Asia are good examples in this area.

Recent centuries saw the introduction of financial securities such as stocks, bonds, and derivatives into the financial market. In addition, investment firms provide many options for investors to choose from, such as mutual funds, stock options, derivatives, commodities and foreign currencies, etc. However, all investment options carry with them varying degrees of risk. Not long ago, as a result of the financial crisis, the Dow Jones Index dropped from over 13,000 in 2008 to 7,000 in 2009. The total worth of financial assets was reduced 45%. At the time, many people joked that their 401K retirement funds had become "201Ks." It made a devastating impact on many people at or close to retirement age. Nevertheless, programs such as 401Ks, traditional IRAs, and Roth IRAs are designated by the U.S. government to encourage saving for retirement and come with significant tax advantages. They should be among the first choices for those Americans wanting to invest funds for their retirement.

Many Chinese Americans, in particular those with corporate jobs, have expanded their investment portfolios to include these areas. Some have even become professional fund managers on Wall Street managing different securities. Nevertheless, Confucianism-influenced Chinese Americans take a relatively conservative approach to investing. Today, for many Chinese Americans, investing in physical assets, such as real estate, is still their preferred choice, in addition to 401Ks or IRAs. As introduced earlier, in the last three years, as the financial crisis drove down real estate prices, many Chinese Americans started buying houses, condominiums, and other investment properties at foreclosure or other highly discounted prices. In general, they are very prudent in handling their investments. They save on a regular basis. When golden opportunities arise, they typically have the money and resolve to make their move.

#6. Take a Long-Term View; Plan for the Future

Obviously, money management is a challenging endeavor. When you are busy deciding how best to allocate your income for the next day's spending—meals, clothing, utilities, gasoline, auto and property insurance—some sizable spending issues quietly arise: your need to replace the tires on your car and to pay for your family's upcoming summer vacation. After facing this challenge year after year, you reach a place where you find your children are grown and ready to attend college. This step comes with a very high price tag. And it is one that will be due every year for the next four years. As you go through life, more such expenditures are coming: your children's wedding, your retirement, taking care of your aging parents, and so on and so forth. The list can be very long. How to deal with such challenges? You have to develop a forward-looking approach, plan for the future. This is what Confucianism advocates.

Confucius said, "If a person does not think about the future, he must be pre-occupied by near term worries (人无远虑，必有近忧)."[18] Another well-known Chinese four-character idiom teaches that people should always plan for the long term (从长计议). This view is reflected in the Confucian view regarding setting up your career aspiration. It also forms part of the Confucian money management concept. The basic notion of leaving a surplus for the future clearly reflects it.

Confucianism-influenced Chinese American families look ahead to future needs and set aside money on a regular basis. Among future needs, the number one item is their children's education. This includes buying a house in a good school district—a must for almost every Chinese family in America. Ensuring their children get an excellent education is their first priority. In pursuit of this objective, the expenses will mount in the development of children's skills, intellectual and otherwise: musical, dancing, the arts, and sports. In most cases, the children will stand out in school and be participants in various science, mathematics, and other competitions. The parents will spend money to support them. Usually, the parents will do their best to save for the children's college education because they do not want to burden their children with a student loan balance.

Investing toward a better career is another key item. In order to advance their careers, many Chinese Americans will spend the money and time it takes to get a professional certification or an advanced degree. If the original career path does not yield good opportunities for upward movement, many Chinese Americans choose to get more education in a new field in order to move into a more promising profession.

Saving for retirement is another major investment for most Chinese families in the US. Most Chinese Americans do not place their full faith in Social Security and Medicare. They do not believe they will be able to draw full benefits when they reach retirement age. As preparation for that day, they work hard, save all they can, and make investments. As I introduced earlier, 401Ks, IRAs, and real estate are among the top options for their retirement investment.

After planning for these predictable future items, Confucianism-influenced Chinese American families will still save extra for uncertainties. This is money that can be used to deal with unpredictable mishaps in life, such as loss of a job in an economic downturn or serious illness/injury.

Overall, thanks to thousands years of Confucian influence, most Chinese American families utilize a long-term view and a conservative approach to dealing with money management. These are the cornerstones on which many Chinese Americans gradually build their wealth in this land to realize their American Dream.

#7 Be Good at Money Management

Another cornerstone of successful Chinese American money management is the acquisition of money management knowledge and skills. These are very important, particularly for those living in the US. You need to have basic money management skills in order to deal with investment and make major purchasing decisions. As we discussed earlier, many modern investment choices can be very involved or complicated, such as stocks, bonds, mutual funds, and derivatives. In order to find a right balance between financial return and risk exposure, you need to have some basic knowledge of investment. At the very least you need to know which high-risk securities to avoid. You may say to yourself, *I do not need that kind of knowledge. I can get a good broker to handle my financial investment.* But in the US, a decision such as buying a house or even a car requires some understanding of money management. When you buy a house, just the settlement statement contains dozens of lines of financial numbers. If you do not know which items deserve your strict attention and how to add them up, you may end up losing your home a few years down the road, just like millions of unfortunate American families did in the last three years.

In addition, you need basic money management skills to keep from falling into the traps set by greedy telemarketers and financial predators. A compelling example is the mortgage market before the financial crisis, when many lenders aggressively sold adjustable rate mortgages and even "balloon loans." (In the initial years of repaying a balloon loan the borrower pays only a small amount, a flat fee. Years later, the borrower has to pay the entire outstanding balance.) A lot of borrowers got locked into such loans without fully understanding the risks associated with them. Former mortgage lender Countrywide was able to sell adjustable rate mortgages to about 49% of its customers. (Some of the loans sold by Countrywide were very high-risk "pay option ARM" loans in which the principle balance could grow over the time if borrowers elected to pay only the minimum payment.)[19] Unfortunately too many of them ended up in foreclosure, which in turn led to the bankruptcy of Countrywide. As another example, consider the many credit card offers you receive in the mail. They offer you the choice of a balance transfer, promising a rebate of 3% while charging 14.9% APR on the outstanding balance. However, unless you cannot pay off the recurring balance on another card with a much higher interest rate, you should avoid walking into such a trap. This is simply because although you get a 3% rebate, you end up paying the bank 11.9% (14.9% minus 3%) in one year. The net result is you giving away your money to the bank. On the retail marketing side, many consumers are attracted to stores by offers of "$10 off when you make a $50 purchase." If you really need something, that could be a good bargain. If not, you end up paying for stuff you do not need. In reality, it is simply a way for retailers to lure you into their stores. Likewise you should never believe this kind slogan: "The more you buy, the more you save." The only truth about shopping is this: "The more you buy, the more you spend!"

Confucianism-influenced Chinese Americans are relatively immune to such "monetary viruses" because they emphasize education, in particular math education. I belong to the wave of Chinese immigrants who came to the US after China implemented its Open and Reform Policy in the 1980s. When I landed in the US, I was perplexed by how stores tended to mark prices as $9.99, $19.99, and $99.99 or another round number minus 1 cent. So I asked my American friends. Finally, someone told me that it was invented by shrewd businessmen in order to give consumers the impression that a product selling at $99.99 had been priced at under $100, thus falling below a psychological watermark in the mind of consumers. I was amazed to learn that some American consumers could be misled by such a pricing scheme. Most Chinese round up $99.99 or even $95 to $100. If you go to China, you will find most products are priced in round numbers—¥10, ¥20, or ¥100—because most consumers understand the basic math and will not be misled by the illusion that $99 is significantly below $100. It really isn't!

Being good at math will help lay a good foundation for understanding money management. It is also mandatory in Chinese culture to teach the next generation about money management. In every Chinese family, the parents will ask the children to learn how to handle their money affairs (会算账). I had a relative, Mr. He Qianzu, who lived in Luquan, a county near Kunming, Yunnan Province. He was not allowed to pursue an education during China's Cultural Revolution because he was born from a landlord's family. All he could write was his name, and his family taught him the simple method of counting money such as was needed to keep track of income and spending. This was at a level similar to elementary algebra. After Deng Xiaoping implemented China's economic reform in the early 1980s, he started a construction business and managed his money wisely. By the early 1990s, he was the richest person in the whole county. From this example, you can see the power of managing your money wisely.

It is fair to say: If you have a good understanding of elementary mathematics, you should be able to handle income and expense issues. If you have a grasp of middle or high school level mathematics, you should be able to understand complex purchasing decisions such as those involved in taking out a car loan or mortgage financing. In order to obtain a good understanding of various investment securities, you may need a college degree or some special training in this area. One should not underestimate the disadvantage of being weak in mathematics. If you do not have a good handle on it, you will never be considered for any highly paid engineering jobs. If you do not have a basic grasp of it, you will have difficulty with money management and become vulnerable to financial predators.

As we discussed in Chapter 5, most Chinese American families treat education as a passion. They make every effort to enable their children to go to good colleges. This lays a good foundation for their money management. With this kind of foundation, they extend their traditional money management concepts such as saving and long-term planning into many of the modern areas created by Western society, such as buying appropriate insurance to protect your wealth and investing in stocks, mutual funds, and other securities.

As shown in the chart below, under the influence of Confucianism, most Chinese American families are creating a virtuous circle in their money management: Thrift + Long-term View => Saving + Good Education => Higher Income + Good Money Management Skills => Increased Wealth Generation!

This approach is far superior to the approach taken by many unsuccessful American families: Overspend + Short-term View => No Saving + Poor Education => Low Income + Poor Money Management Skills => More Financial Challenges. It is a vicious circle that is best completely avoided!

Chart 8. Two Different Paths of Money Management

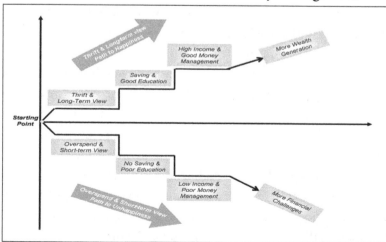

Chapter 7

FOURTH VALUE: *GU-JIA* (顾家)

"Caring for Your Family"—Confucian Value of Creating Harmonized, Happy, and Progressive Families

7.1 THE IMPORTANCE OF CARING FOR YOUR FAMILY IN TODAY'S AMERICAN SOCIETY

Family is the most important building block of a society. When you are young, the family provides the shelter, love, care, and nurturing for you to grow up to become a successful adult. When you reach a mature age, the family you formed is the place where you and your loved one care for each other, give mutual love and support mentally, physically, and economically, and raise children together. When you are old, the family you nurtured, your spouse, your children and grandchildren, will provide you with joy, love, and care, which are essential for your happiness after your retirement. Happy families lead to happy lives.

137

A happy family typically has two characteristics. The first is stability, and the second is success. In a stable family, the husband and wife do not have to spend time, energy, and money constantly at odds and in pursuit of separation, divorce, and other options destructive to the family. As a result, they devote their love, care, and economic resources to the family, to support each other, to raise the children, and/or to care for the elderly. In a successful family, in addition to family stability, there is constant love between family members, clearly defined roles and responsibilities, and good family management. In such a family, the safety and health of family members are protected and managed, the behavior of family members is properly guided, and the career development and life skills of family members are well prepared.

In the 21st century, building and maintaining a stable and healthy family still poses a significant challenge for many Americans. Between 40% and 50% of marriages will end up in divorce. Each year, over one million American children suffer the divorce of their parents. More than half of the children born in the US will see their parents divorce before they turn 18. According to a host of research published in scientific journals, failed marriages are likely to cause plights for the children of divorce:[1]

- They become increasingly the victims of abuse and neglect. They tend to have more health, behavioral, and emotional problems and stand a greater chance of being involved in crime, drug abuse, and even suicide.
- They tend to have a reduced learning capacity, have poorer academic performance at school, and become dropouts.
- There tends to be a significant drop in household income, which leads to a poorer living standard for the children. According to research published in 1993, "four times as many divorced women with children fell under the poverty line [as did] married women with children."[2]

Divorce not only causes irreparable hardship for children, but also leads to significant emotional, economic, and social suffering for the spouses. It creates emotional stress, even depression, that can severely impact a person's job performance and other activities. On the economic side, the legal costs associated with getting a divorce can range from minimal, if the parties can reach an agreement on the division of assets and custody of the children, to exorbitant, if a fundamental dispute over property or custody is involved. It could take years and many thousands of dollars depending on the complexity of the case and the willingness of both parties to compromise. Even after the divorce has been settled, both parties have to live apart, paying two separate mortgages/rents and two sets of utility bills, in effect doubling the cost of housing. Furthermore, if there are children involved, additional effort will be required to schedule visitation and coordinate the children's activities. What are the costs to society? Each year the federal government spends $150 billion to subsidize single-parent families.[3]

As we have moved into the 21st century, we should not stigmatize divorce or label it taboo, not when it can serve those couples that have genuinely irreconcilable differences. Tragically, many couples break up because of an inability to handle a marriage relationship or because they are insufficiently prepared to handle the challenges that come with forming a family. The more people can improve their knowledge and skills in handling family affairs, the less chance they will end up in divorce. Individual couples will have an improved capacity to build more stable families and society will need to expend less money and effort on taking care of poor, broken families.

In addition to divorced families, there are a lot of stable, but unsuccessful American families that suffer various social, health, and legal problems. Among them, the biggest health challenge facing Americans has to do with their weight. As I cited in Chapter 1, today, two-thirds of all adults and about a third of all children and teenagers in the US are either overweight or obese. It is predicted that 70% of obese adolescents will become obese adults. What are the health impacts of obesity? It leads to a higher rate of heart disease, diabetes, high blood pressure, and many chronic diseases that entail the leading causes of American deaths. The direct medical costs related to obesity in the US, according to an estimate, were $147 billion in 2008. It is a significant burden to both society and individual families. If future Medicaid/ Medicare benefits are reduced, as many predict, the financial burden on many American families will be too heavy to bear.

Many American families also suffer from other social problems, including alcohol and drug abuse. It is estimated that the total deaths per year caused by alcohol number around 23,000 whereas those caused by drug abuse number around 37,500.[4] Many young lives are lost to such social maladies. Some adolescents even get involved in drug trafficking and gangs. Although the US is among the richest countries in the world, our crime rate is among the highest in the world. Although these issues may appear to be social and legal in nature and families the victims, many studies have demonstrated that failed families and childhood neglect and abuse are contributing factors to youths becoming criminals.

It is fair to say that while obesity, drug abuse, and crime all have social and economic causes, families can play an important role in managing or preventing these latencies from manifesting. If more families improve their family management skills, bringing more love, attention, and discipline to their family members, they can significantly reduce such problems, making their families healthier and happier. If more families are better managed, society as a whole will become safer and better.

7.2 THE CONFUCIAN VALUE OF *GU-JIA* (顾家): CARING FOR YOUR FAMILY

Caring for and properly managing families is a cornerstone of Confucianism and an essential part of the political-social value systems established by Confucius and his followers. Aimed at building a society in which people are treated appropriately and humanely, Confucianism has established norms—moral standards for both politicians and family members to follow. In the mind of Confucius, the family is as important as the nation, and a prerequisite to becoming a successful politician is the ability to manage the family and have sufficient self-discipline. There are four key elements of Confucian family values.

1. Properly define the social and ethical norms to be followed by the family members

In "Ten Human Duties (十义)" as described in the Confucian classic, the *Book of Rites*, the first six duties are used to define the family relationships:[5]

(1) *Fu-ci* (父慈): The father/parent should be devoted to and love their children.

(2) *Zi-xiao* (子孝): The children should respect and care for their parents.

(3) *Fu-he* (夫和): The husband should treat his wife well.

(4) *Qi-shun* (妻顺) *: The wife should support her husband's decisions.

(5) *Xiong-you* (兄友): The elder brother/sibling should treat the younger brother/sibling friendly.

(6) *Di-gong* (弟恭) *: The younger brother/sibling should treat the elder brother/sibling with respect.

As you can see, the first six of the "Ten Human Duties" address the key relationships in the family: parent-children, husband-wife, and sibling-sibling. In this way, family members have clearly defined rules to follow. Social norms were also used to resolve interpersonal conflicts and disputes. They helped in creating harmonized family relationships and maintaining family stability.

2. Use humanism (Ren) in conducting interpersonal relationships

Contrary to the view held by many critics of Confucianism, all of the "Ten Human Duties" were defined in a mutually beneficial way so that social norms would apply to both parties in the relationship. For example, the definition of the parent-children relationship asks not only that the children respect and care for their parents, but also that the parents love their children. Similarly, it calls for the older sibling(s)

---

* As I pointed out in Chapter 3, traditional Confucian social norms, created 2,500 years ago, are not without their shortcomings, which include unequivocal treatment of women and children. These values have been abandoned since the introduction of 20th century Western values.

to treat the younger sibling(s) kindly and the younger sibling(s) to treat the older sibling(s) with respect.

3. Create family harmony[6]

Confucian family behavior guidelines focus on enhancing bonding and creating harmony among all family members. Confucius said that when applying the social norms, creating harmony is the first priority (礼之用，和为贵).[7] This is particularly true when handling family affairs. In Chinese society, "family harmony leads to the success of all family agendas (家和万事兴)" is one of most popular phrases used from generation to generation in guiding family affairs. Today, family harmony (家庭和睦) is still the central theme within Chinese families in China and abroad.

4. Actively mange the family[8]

In one of the four classics of Confucianism, *Great Learning*, the concept of "managing family (齐家, *qi-jia*)" is introduced as an essential quality in order to become a successful statesman. In the Confucian view, the father should take a leading role in managing the family: establishing and implementing family discipline, managing interpersonal relationships, maintaining the stability of the family, and achieving family objectives toward honor and prosperity.

Confucian family values have had widespread influence in China. In Chinese society, family is regarded as the most important social unit and the focus of family members. In ancient China, every family that could afford it had a designated room or place to worship their ancestors. Family rules and norms were established to regulate relationships in the family and ensure proper family tradition would be sustained to lead the family. The father or the eldest son is put in charge to manage the family, to ensure the young are raised properly, the seniors taken care of, and the offspring put on a path in which they continue to uphold family tradition and bring honor and prosperity to the family. If a family member succeeds in his career, becoming a government official or a successful businessman, he will be honored by his own family and his extended family. If a child strays from the family tradition and brings shame to the family, he will be severely punished or even expelled from the family. In ancient China, family did not serve merely as a shelter that provided warmth, food, and happiness for each of its members. The family also had its collective mission: to strive to make the family successful, one generation after another!

Well defined social norms and ethical stands, harmony, active family management, as well as an emphasis on the humane approach to treating interpersonal relationships are the cornerstones of Confucian family values. They have led to family stability and progress for many Chinese families and contributed to the formation of an orderly and prosperous society in China. Clearly such values compose one of the driving factors that has enabled ancient China to become one of the most prosperous nations in the world for over 2,000 years.

As I discussed in Chapter 3, in the last two centuries, China has also been impacted by the influence of modern Western values, noticeably in the areas of women's rights and the equal treatment of youths in the family. As a result, many changes have taken place in Chinese family structure: Most urban families and increasingly more rural families have reformed their household structure from the traditionally three-generational type to the modern nuclear family type in which parents and unmarried children live together. Patriarchal family management is no longer the default social norm. Depending on their capability, more and more females are becoming the head of the family and take charge of family management. Youths have been empowered to air their opinions more freely in the family and make more decisions. Individuality has become increasingly recognized and respected in Chinese families.

Nevertheless, based on thousands of years of civilization, most Chinese families still maintain many valuable family traditions, combining modern Western values into their Confucian cultural heritage. As it turns out, this kind of "secular Confucianism" approach to family values releases significant strengths that have helped a lot of Chinese families succeed in China and overseas. *This is the fourth Chinese secret for success: Caring for your family to create love, harmony and success.*

In the following section, I will share with you how modern Chinese American families apply these values in their daily lives.

7.3 HOW CHINESE FAMILIES USE *GU-JIA* (顾家) TO MANAGE THEIR FAMILIES SUCCESSFULLY

#1 Devotion to Family Happiness

Across various ethnic groups, the Chinese are among those who care most for their families. Many family members are willing to make an extra effort or even sacrifice to achieve this mission. In today's urban China and the US, you may not see many Chinese families that still designate a room or space to worship their ancestors. However, their devotion toward their families has not diminished. They simply focus more on their immediate family members—their children, spouse, and parents.

This value is also shared by many other Confucianism-influenced Asian American families. According to the Pew Research Center, 67% of Asian Americans believe that being a good parent is "one of the most important things" in their lives while only 50% of all American adults agree. Similarly, more Asian Americans value a successful marriage (54%) as "one of the most important things in life" than the general population (34%).[9]

Devotion to their children, in particular their career development, is the number one priority in most Chinese families. This is what Michelle Kwan's parents did. As mentioned in Chapter 4, as a middle class family, her parents devoted all their efforts and money to support her and her sister Karen in pursuing their figure-skating dream. They even went so far as to sell their house in order to pay their training costs.[10]

The career of world-famous Chinese pianist Lang Lang is another touching example of parental devotion to their children's future. After discovering Lang Lang's musical talent when he was two years old, his father, Lang Guo, was determined to make him into a world-class pianist. He made an extraordinary effort to support Lang Lang in developing his talents. He searched for the best tutors for Lang

Lang, assisting them in organizing and monitoring the practice sessions for his son. When Lang Lang was nine, his father made a major sacrifice, quitting his job to accompany Lang Lang when he relocated to attend a top-ranked music school in Beijing, 500 miles south of their hometown of Shenyang. That decision initiated a long period of hardship for Lang Lang's parents. His father spent all his time taking care of him in Beijing while his mother worked hard in Shenyang, saving every penny to support the family. Fortunately, this extraordinary sacrifice paid off. Eight years later, Lang Lang won a number of world competitions and in August 1999 gave a career-changing performance at the Ravinia Festival of Chicago, where he was chosen to fill in for the world-famous musician Andre Watts, thereafter basking in the world's classical music spotlight.[11]

Michelle Kwan and Lang Lang's stories are not uncommon in Chinese culture. For some professions that require an extraordinary effort such as music, sports, and gymnastics, the parents typically do everything in their power to support their children. For families with a limited income, it is common to see the parents, sisters, and brothers all saving money to support an especially promising child in their college or study-abroad endeavor. This is what happened in my family, my sister's family, and almost every Chinese family I know.

The selfless sacrifice of parents plants a deep-rooted "seed of love" in the soil of many Chinese families. This reflects a core family value of Confucianism, *fu-ci* (父慈): The father/parent should be devoted to and love their children. When the parents get old, the children have more affection for them. They are more willing to respect and give back to their parents, and care for them. This is another key family value of Confucianism, called *zi-xiao* (子孝). The parents' devotion to the children and the children's care for the elderly creates a stronger vertical bonding than that found in families in some other cultures, which emphasize primarily horizontal bonding, the husband-wife relationship.

The horizontal bonding found in Confucianism-influenced Chinese families is also emphasized. In the 1980s and 1990s, many poor Chinese students came to the US for graduate study. Constrained by their financial situations, many Chinese couples made sacrifices to help each other: First they devote the time and money to help one spouse to get the education s/he wants. Next, after s/he has landed a good job, they turn their attention to the other spouse, helping him/her to get a good education and find a job. This was the case with me and with many of my Chinese friends. They use a similar approach in handling many other issues such as health, hobbies, and achieving their family goals one by one.

What makes Chinese family devotion stand out is the extraordinary pursuit of a family mission: to make the family successful, one generation after another. If the parents come from a poor background, they will be highly motivated to enable their children to achieve better lives than they had. This motivates them to make sacrifices. If the parents come from an affluent background, they will be highly motivated to ensure their children can maintain it. This motivates them to put a lot of effort toward educating their children, just like what "Tiger Mom" did.

If we apply business management principles to analyzing the Chinese family approach, we will find it to be efficient and effective. It views the family as an organization with clear organizational objectives, and it optimizes the resources of the organization to achieve its objectives. If we look at the example of Michelle Kwan, in terms of the money her parents invested, it was far less than what she achieved after she won the world championship and had established her career.

Lang Lang's example is very similar. His parents sacrificed about eight years worth of a single-person salary in exchange for a thrifty life for the family and expending an extraordinary amount of time and effort to support Lang Lang as he studied in Beijing. In so doing, they enabled Lang Lang to become a world famous pianist, ensured a happy life for Lang Lang, and enabled millions of dollars of income for Lang Lang and the family. The monetary investment—Lang Guo's eight years worth of salary—totaled well below US$500,000. The return on the investment, measured in both monetary and emotional terms, was very high.

Take as another example that of "Tiger Mom" Amy Chua. Although the parenting approach she took with her two daughters is debatable, the results she achieved with her family are quite outstanding: Both she and her husband are Yale Law School professors. Her husband is also a bestselling novelist. She authored two bestsellers before publishing the "Tiger Mom" book. On the top of that, she successfully trained her two daughters to become an exceptional pianist and an outstanding young violinist, with excellent academic performance and fluency in Chinese.[12] There is no question the achievements her family has realized are remarkable and could not have been possible had the family not worked together toward the same goal.

In contrast, in individualistic overly driven families, the family acts more as a shelter, with each family member more focused on his/her individual interests and the family objective centered around making everybody comfortable and ensuring they all have a high degree of freedom. Under this circumstance, because the norms and expectations for individual devotion to the family are relatively low, family members are likely to argue if his/her interests are violated or if s/he is asked to put forth an effort on behalf of other family members. In this way, families make themselves vulnerable to any significant challenges they may face. Many families are unable to survive in the long run, and therefore, stand little chance to meet with success.

Clearly one must strive for a good balance between Confucianism, which stresses collectivism in the family, and Western culture, which stresses individualism in the family. At the end of this chapter I will discuss how to combine the strengths of both cultures to reach an optimal degree of family devotion.

#2 Define Proper Roles, and Behavior Guidance for Family Members

A family is a social organization. Like a business, it needs to define proper roles, processes/social norms, and behavior guidance. With proper roles defined, the adults, husband and wife, will have established an appropriate division of labor to take the lead roles in the family. The juniors, in return, will know what they need to do and to whom they should turn on specific issues. Although in a family setting it is very difficult to have clear-cut roles and responsibilities defined, it is essential to ensuring a basic structure is in place. Otherwise, it leaves a lot of gray areas, which have the potential to cause disputes between the spouses and confusion among the children.

In the traditional practice of Confucianism, the husband/father assumes the role as head of the household (一家之长). He takes care of external affairs such as education and career matters while the wife/mother takes care of internal affairs such as housekeeping and interpersonal relationships among family members (男主外、女主内). In terms of family role play, a "strict father and caring mother (严父慈母)" approach is regarded as the best parenting model in most Chinese families. In this model, the father establishes authority in order to educate and enforce good discipline in the children. He focuses more on the children's schooling and ethical behavior. In contrast, the mother oversees the nutrition, health, and psychological development of the children and performs a bonding function in the family. If the father overplays the strict side, the mother will provide psychological compensation, consoling the children. If the mother treats the children too leniently, the father can exert his influence and bring more discipline to the children. In essence, this is a highly effective collaborative parenting mechanism that provides both discipline and love to the children. To varying degrees, many successful cultures adopt similar approaches in their parenting practices. Many contemporary studies indicate that absence of a paternal influence in a family leads to significantly higher crime rates in the children, clearly illustrating the importance of discipline in a family.

Confucianism also defines the roles and responsibilities of the children. The eldest or smartest son is typically designated to succeed the family head. He is trained to be objective and to lead and to take care of his younger siblings. All the children are expected to show respect to their parents and their older brothers/sisters and to love one another.

As mentioned in a previous section, the Confucian guidelines for interpersonal behavior of family members are defined in the first six of the "Ten Human Duties (十义)" from the *Book of Rites* (礼记).

Following these guidelines, most Chinese families have set up even more detailed rules of behavior for their family members. Typically it has been established by the founder or first knowledgeable head of the family, who summarized his experience in managing his family in a document to be passed from one generation to the next, such as "Family Tree (家谱)," "Family Rules (家规)," or "Family Teachings (家训)."

One of the most famous sets of family behavior rules were written by Zhu Yong Chun (朱用纯,1627–1698) in his masterpiece, *Zhu-Zi's Family Teaching*《朱子家训》.[13] It makes concise use of 500 characters to cover almost every aspect of family management:

- Get up early, close doors and windows before going to bed.
- Clean the house daily and keep kitchen utensils clean.
- Be thrifty on a daily basis; no lavish banquets.
- Plan for rainy days.
- Respect your ancestors and care for your parents.
- Educate the children.
- Be modest, not greedy.
- Be nice to others; do not take advantage of small business vendors.
- Be generous with the poor and the weak; do not take advantage of them.
- Treat all family members fairly.
- Do not be flattering with the rich; do not be condescending with the poor.
- Do not socialize with people who behave badly.
- When receiving a complaint, give the matter some thought before responding.
- When involved in a dispute, check your side of the story first.
- Do not concern yourself with the help you've given others; but keep in mind the help other people have given you…

Since its publication, *Zhu-Zi's Family Teaching* has become very popular in China. In 2007, when I visited the historic village of

Hong Cun, located underneath the beautiful Huangshan Mountain in Anhui Province, I found *Zhu-Zi's Family Teaching* had been used by the local school as a guide for students well into the 20th century.

In the context of an ancient society, these behavior guidelines established the moral standards for family members to follow to maintain a mutually beneficial family structure, led by a caring and authoritative father/husband. They emphasize rules that prevent family members from engaging in behavior that may be destructive to the family. They also ask children to confront the parents if they engage in improper behavior. It requires younger generations to study hard, develop sound skills, and make meaningful achievements.

In modern Chinese society and Chinese American families, the roles and responsibilities are no longer as rigid as they once were. Depending on the capability of the spouses, in some families the wife/mother assumes the role as the head of the family. If she is successful in handling careers and education, the wife usually takes charge of handling external affairs. The spouses play more equal roles when it comes to decision making. However, the head of household concept still exists in most cases. In general, the more capable one takes this important position. The "strict father, caring mother" parenting model still applies to most Chinese families, although sometimes, depending on the personalities of the husband and wife, the roles may be reversed, as we see in the case of "Tiger Mom" Amy Chua, in which she plays the role of "strict mother." In the meantime, the children's interests and ideas receive more respect. If in ancient times Chinese parents tended to use an "authoritarian" approach (parents dictate most decision making for the children) in their parenting, then today most Chinese American families use an "authoritative" approach, one of the most successful approaches recognized by modern sociologists. In this approach, the parents create an authoritative influence. At the same time, they explain to the children the reasoning behind their decisions so the children will learn how to make similar decisions. They combine a high degree of parental influence with communication aimed at enhancing their children's understanding. While the older children are still required to take care of the younger ones, siblings are typically asked to share in the household responsibilities. In modern Chinese American families, many valuable concepts of Confucianism still prevail. They include:

- The definition of the roles and responsibilities among family members;
- The leadership role of the head of household;
- The presence of a modified, flexible "strict father, caring mother" parenting model;
- The definition of elder brother/sister roles and responsibilities.

With regard to the behavior guidelines, today most Chinese families still follow a lot of the rules regarding social behavior although they have become less formal. Some are written down and agreed to by the family members such as a "Dos and Don'ts" list for children in order to make sure they study as expected and avoid bad influences. More importantly, knowingly or unknowingly, most of them follow a set of unwritten rules that are deeply rooted, passed from one generation to the next. After taking into account good Western values like respect for women and individual development, many valuable Confucianism guidelines are still benefiting Chinese families, such as:

- *Gu-jia* (顾家): Caring for the family.
- *Fu-ci* (父慈): The father/parent should be devoted to and love their children.
- *Zi-xiao* (子孝): The children should respect and care for their parents.
- *Fu-qi-he-mu* (夫妻和睦): Harmony should exist between husband and wife.
- *Xiong-di-jie-mei-you-ai* (兄弟姐妹友爱): Siblings should have a friendly relationship.
- *Yao shang-jin, zeng-qi* (要上进、争气): One should make an effort to progress one's career or family.
- *Bu-ke duo-luo, bai-jia* (不可堕落、败家): One should stay away from bad or destructive behaviors that may ruin the family.

These family-oriented guidelines set up a high moral standard for the family members. They require that each adult be a contributing member of the family. They are expected to love the family and be willing to make necessary sacrifices on behalf of the family. With regard to children's responsibility, today's retirement system has eliminated the need for the younger generation to repay the parents economically. However, most Chinese families have never wavered in their expectation for the junior family members to develop their living skills and to be successful and bring honor and happiness to the family. This is an essential part of the family guidelines for almost every Chinese family. As you can see, Chinese family guidelines have two clear objectives:

(1) Regulate interpersonal relationships; encourage family bonding and stability.
(2) Orient the family to succeed.

With the roles and responsibilities thus defined, and following the family-oriented guidelines, many Chinese American families have laid a solid foundation to steer the family on a stable and successful journey.

#3 Actively Manage the Family

Managing the family (齐家, qi-jia) is introduced in one of the four classics of Confucianism, *Great Learning*. In its original concept, managing the family is the second of four stages of personal cultivation: self-discipline, managing the family, administrating the state, and bringing peace to the world.

As Confucianism spread to Chinese society and become secular, the purpose of managing the family expanded and became more relevant to family happiness. This includes managing the wellbeing of family members, avoiding family setbacks or mishaps, and setting up and achieving family objectives to become prosperous and successful, generation after generation. *Zhu-Zi's Family Teaching*, which I introduced in an earlier section, provides a glimpse of such family management. Its scope is very comprehensive.

In ancient times, the typical Chinese family consisted of three generations living under one roof. That arrangement led to complex family relationships and made family management a daunting task. Today, most Chinese American families have adopted the nuclear family format, with a husband and wife living with unmarried children, in which the challenges of family management have been significantly reduced. However, active family management is still an outstanding strength of Confucianism-influenced Chinese families.

As a comparison, in many unsuccessful families, active management is absent. The members take a passive attitude, with each of them concerned with offering only minimal support to the family. Their concept of family does not go beyond the idea of it being a shelter or roof under which they all live together. In such a family one spouse may refrain from intervening when the other spouse begins to gain weight to an unhealthy degree. If a child in such a family falls behind in school, the parents may make no significant effort to step in and help the child succeed academically. Likewise the parents may fail to erect a firewall to vigorously prevent bad influences such as drugs or gang behavior from reaching their child.

Confucianism-influenced families, on the other hand, take a much more aggressive approach in managing family matters. Their focus, which does not shift, is to make the family stable and successful.

1. Maintain family stability

In order to maintain family stability, as introduced earlier, Confucianism set up a high moral standard in requiring couples to devote more of themselves to the family. Such parental devotion helps to create a strong emotional bond in the family. Besides, Confucianism has also developed many rich values to create family harmony, such as *tolerance, yielding,* and *self-control,* which will be introduced in the next section. These values and practices illustrate the proactive side of marriage management.

On the reactive side, due largely to cultural reasons, Confucianism-influenced Chinese families widely view divorce as an undesirable solution. Of greatest concern here is the negative impact it stands to have on the children. Most Chinese parents feel shameful or guilty when a marriage fails, in particular for the inability to maintain an intact family, which is essential for the wellbeing and proper development of their children. The marriage bond is a major fence in the protection of the family.

The influence of parents and extended family members is the second fence. If the couple is having a dispute, the natural reaction from their parents is to ask why they cannot work things out. In most cases they will step in, try to persuade the couple to save the marriage unless the dispute is irreconcilable or the love bond has been irreparably broken. Confucianism-influenced Chinese families use many other common approaches to deal with family crises and maintain family stability. The results are astonishing. In many U.S. classrooms, the children of Chinese American parents are often the only ones who have an intact family. This is particularly true for those whose parents are first generation immigrants. As previously mentioned, the divorce rate for Chinese Americans is about 3.8%, much lower than that of the overall American population: 9.7%.[14]

2. Pursue family success

Confucianism-influenced Chinese families do not stop at maintaining a stable family. They want the family to be successful. In order to achieve and maintain a successful family, they manage three important areas:

The first is the education of the children. As we already discussed in Chapter 5, this is always the focus of the family. Successful education leads to a better, more secure future for the children. It also leads to a sense of pride and happiness for the family. Although Chinese people tend to be modest, they are never shy about telling friends or neighbors about their children's accomplishments. This is the most important measure of family success for most Chinese families.

The second is the moral development of family members. This is essential for preventing the family members, especially juniors, from crossing over into bad behaviors such as drug abuse, gambling, and crime. In Confucianism-influenced Chinese families, the parents always warn the children not to engage in any bad behaviors, not to fall into "one misstep which may lead to regrets for years to come (一失足，成千古恨)." They build a robust firewall to protect the family members. They are sensitive to what the children read and talk about and whom they make friends with. If there is an early warning sign or a red flag, the parents will take immediate action to stop things from getting worse. In addition to the prevention side, Chinese parents also teach their children about which good behaviors they should follow. Although juniors are the primary audience for ethical education, it applies to adult family members as well. If one spouse engages in undesirable behaviors, the other spouse or mature children will step in to curtail it. As a result of such vigorous family management, crime rate and drug use among Chinese/Asian Americans are among the lowest in the country, about one fourth of the national average.

The third is to take care of the health and safety of family members. Perhaps due to cultural reasons, most Chinese people are not as adventurous as Westerners. The parents typically do not allow their children to engage in injury-prone sports or other high-risk activities. This naturally lowers the risk of accident. Many Chinese American families also aggressively manage the health of family members. They feel ashamed if a family member suffers from a behavior-related health issue such as obesity. They try to keep up with nutrition guidelines to ensure the health of family members. More importantly, they establish and implement strict rules to prevent family members from indulging in unhealthy behaviors. If we look at the statistics, Asian Americans (including Chinese Americans) maintain the lowest rate of obesity among the different racial groups.

In general, a majority of Chinese American families have adopted a broad view of family management. They view almost all issues related to family members as a potential topic of family management: physical and emotional wellbeing, behavior, and education. Partly because they come from a society in which the government and corporations assume relatively few social responsibilities, they feel a responsibility to prevent social issues such as drug abuse and obesity from impacting their families. They are also willing to put forth an extra effort to make up for the shortcomings of public services, such as math and science education in public schools. As a minority group in the US, Chinese Americans, in taking an active and aggressive approach to family management, are able to manage their families towards success.

The story of Gary Locke, former governor of Washington State, Secretary of Commerce, and current American Ambassador to China, is a great example of pursuing family success in the US. When Gary's grandfather arrived in the US, he spoke poor English and had no marketable skills. In order to survive in the US, he took a low-end job as a household servant. However, he did not stop there. He took part of his pay in exchange for English lessons, the minimum requirements for getting a better job in the US. After improving his English skills, he got a job as a chef in a large hospital. He then brought his family to join him in the US and actively managed the members. In the next generation, Gary's aunt and uncle got a good education, becoming a doctor and engineer, respectively. His father joined George Patton's army during World War II and later became a small business owner. Gary, a third-generation immigrant, attended Yale University, later becoming an outstanding Chinese American politician. In his interview with a Chinese magazine in 2012, Gary attributed his family's success to a balanced combination of American and Chinese family management values such as devotion to the family, setting up higher standards, emphasis on education, and devoted work ethic.[15]

In the following sections I will introduce a few distinctive Confucian approaches most Chinese families use to address challenging issues of family management.

#4 Nurture Family Harmony through Tolerance, Yielding, and Self-Control

Managing interpersonal relationships is the most critical task in maintaining the emotional bonding among family members and therefore, a stable family. It typically focuses on the spousal relationship, but it goes beyond that. It also covers parent-child relationships, sibling relationships, and sometimes relationships with extended family members such as grandfathers and grandmothers. A misunderstanding or dispute between family members can not only taint their interpersonal relationship, but also bring unhappiness to surrounding family members.

To address these challenges, Confucianism advocates family harmony. What does family harmony (家庭和睦) mean to the family members? It requires family members to

- Treat each other with good intentions and nice manners;
- Understand and provide reasonable support to each other's objectives;
- Minimize and manage conflicts; and
- Be willing to compromise and find win-win solutions.

As in many other cultures, modern Chinese families advocate that family members treat each other nicely and with good intentions. They also emphasize the importance of communication between family members. Communication is essential to enhancing mutual understanding between family members. It can help reduce or eliminate the disputes caused by misunderstandings. In addition, mutual understanding will help the parties to better prioritize each other's interests and build mutual support, which in turn leads to effective conflict management and compromise.

In many cases, good intentions, nice manners, and communication are not enough to address family conflicts, namely when the disputing parties have strong egos and are self-centric. As early as 2,500 years ago, Confucius had already taken note of this issue. In order to achieve family harmony, Confucianism stresses the importance of *ren-rang* (忍让), which means tolerance, yielding, and self-control.[16]

Ren-rang first means to recognize and tolerate the weaknesses of other family members. Adjusting expectations will help reduce tension greatly. For example, a husband typically expects the wife to be a good cook. After many tries, the wife still may not be able to improve her cooking skills to the level the husband expects. If the husband holds onto his expectations, it will surely create tension and dispute. By lowering his expectations, the tension level will be lowered and a potential conflict avoided. However, *ren-rang* here does not mean we should tolerate destructive behaviors such as drug abuse or avoid asking family members to make improvements in critical areas such as children's academics if they can. I will discuss this further in the next section: Achieve Family Success Through Discipline.

Ren-rang also means "yield," the willingness to overlook some of the demands of your ego and your own self-interest on behalf of other family members. In Confucianism, each person is asked to be willing to give priority to someone else's interests. "Three Word Chant" offers the example of Kong Rong, an offspring of Confucius. When he was only four years old, he was gracious enough to let his siblings eat the pear first (融四岁，能让梨).[17] After being cited in "Three Word Chant," he became a role model for millions of Chinese children. By requiring each family member to aspire to such high moral ground, it eliminates the source of a lot of family conflicts, which often are caused by people competing for personal interests.

In case conflicts arise, Confucianism advocates that family members maintain control of their emotions and temper to avoid escalating the crisis. This is the third meaning of *ren-rang*. It is very important to prevent disputes about trivial issues from spilling over and affecting more important family relationships or agendas. Confucius said the inability to control your temper in regard to small things may spoil your larger agenda (小不忍，则乱大谋).[18] Over many years of Confucian influence, self-control has become a distinctive strength of the Chinese culture. With proper self-control, trivial arguments can be kept from escalating into major disputes. Likewise verbal arguments can be kept from deteriorating into domestic violence. When I lived in Beijing from 2005 to 2007, many Western expatriates told me they were surprised to notice that although Chinese drivers argued fiercely whenever a traffic accident occurred, they rarely saw their arguments deteriorate into violent fighting.

Tolerance, yielding, and self-control are valuable family management approaches in maintaining family harmony and stability. I personally do not believe every broken family needs or deserves to be saved. By appropriately applying these approaches, many "should not be broken" families can be saved. In today's

American society, too many families break up not because of irreconcilable differences, but because they have not learned to live together. One spouse cannot tolerate the other's weaknesses. Neither side is willing to yield to the other side's ego or interests. Or in many cases, a lack of emotion/temper control by one or both parties sends a happy family into a downward spiral that ends in divorce. Once family harmony is lost, the foundation on which to build family success collapses. When a couple focuses its effort and attention on rescuing their relationship—or fighting each other—the chance for them to devote their energy to taking care of the children and preparing for their future is very slim.

#5 Achieve Family Success Through Discipline

Domestic harmony is the foundation for family stability. To achieve family success requires even more.

In previous chapters, we introduced the Confucian values of Determination for a Better Life (*li-zhi*), Emphasize Education (*qin-xue*), and Saving (*jie-jian*). All are essential elements of successful family management. In addition to these core values, emphasizing discipline is another distinctive Confucian family management approach. It includes the following features:

1. Embrace behavior guidelines that clearly define right and wrong

Impacted by celebrity-centered pop culture among other factors, the emphasis on moral development has quietly receded in the American mass media and in many families. For example, some criminal suspects and people who chronically misbehave are rewarded with large book deals. When celebrities die of drug abuse or other personal missteps, there rarely is a discussion of the larger lesson to be learned from their tragedies. The line separating right from wrong has become severely blurred.

On the contrary, Confucian family management emphasize on a clear definition of what is right, what is wrong, which behaviors are desirable, and which behaviors are undesirable. These behavior guidelines are sufficiently communicated to give family members a clear direction to pursue good things, to embrace desirable behaviors, and to avoid bad things and undesirable behaviors. On one hand, family members are prohibited from engaging in destructive behaviors such as drug addiction. In most Chinese societies, a visit by a policeman is typically perceived as an indication of bad behavior because in their view, people who behave well should have no run-ins with the law. Social or legal problems are viewed as bad or undesirable things that are best avoided. On the other hand, success and achievement are looked upon with high regard by Confucianism-influenced Chinese families. Children are encouraged to study hard to achieve excellent academic performance. Husband and wife are encouraged to advance their careers. In this way, Confucianism-influenced Chinese families create a strong sense of pride around those things family members should focus on and shame around those things the family members should avoid.

Living across two cultures, I noticed that the Chinese culture and Chinese language still maintain a strong moral orientation that help Chinese in defining behavior guidelines. For example, "illicit drugs" are called, literally, "poisoning products (毒品)." Therefore, "drug abuse" is called "inhale poison (吸毒)" in Chinese. This kind of explicit labeling clearly indicates it is a terrible behavior people should avoid.

I believe most conservative American families, like Confucianism-influenced Asian American families, also exercise distinctive value judgments. Sadly, there are those in the US who fail to impose a strong moral orientation in their families, not realizing that it could benefit their lives. Some do not realize that, in some ways, solving social issues also falls under family responsibility. If the children fall prey to bad influences such as obesity, smoking, or alcohol or drug abuse, some parents, instead of disciplining the children for having developed bad habits, blame fast-food restaurants, cigarette vendors, or a lack of rehab facilities. Clearly, society as a whole should push fast-food restaurants to sell healthier food and the government to limit cigarette sales. But it is parents who have the main responsibility to impress upon their children the virtues of avoiding bad influences.

2. Hold your family members to high standards

When disciplining their children, some people confuse "family tolerance" with "social tolerance." In so doing they lower their standards for their family members. It is true that every individual has equal rights and should be treated equally. For example, society should not discriminate politically against someone for being overweight or for having developed a drug addiction. However, responsible parents should make a reasonable effort to prevent obesity or drug addition from developing in a family member. The level of "family tolerance" should be much lower than "social tolerance" for the same issue because parents are responsible for the wellbeing of their children; a similar responsibility exists between spouses. Although it may be inappropriate to urge an overweight neighbor to lose weight, it is reasonable to demand your children watch what they eat and make them aware that obesity is undesirable and signals a lack of self-discipline. It may be okay that the government or society does not impose moral standards on individuals. However, if a family lacks or loosens its moral standards, it may lead to failure of the family, owing to drug abuse, violence, or worse.

In contrast, Confucianism-influenced Chinese families apply high standards to their family management. It is a fundamental obligation for parents to teach their children about social norms and behavior guidelines and impose strict requirements on their family members. This is called family cultivation (家庭教养, *jia-ting-jiao-yang*) in Chinese society. In many dangerous areas such as drugs, gambling, and gang violence, Confucianism-influenced families do not allow the children to make such mistakes in the hopes they will learn from them. They simply forbid their children from associating with people displaying such behaviors in the first place. When dealing with regular behavior issues, Confucianism asks that parents be stricter on their children than on others.

When I was young, whenever my sister, brother, or I got into a dispute with other children, my parents always held us to a higher standard. The first thing they did was ask if we had done something wrong to cause the dispute. We did not always understand why our parents questioned us first before looking to the other children like other parents did. I did not realize the approach they took was deeply rooted in Confucian teaching until I learned more about Confucianism later on. Confucius said, "If you are willing to blame yourself more than others [when a dispute arises], it will avoid hatred from others (躬自厚而薄责于人，则远怨矣)."[19] This kind of self-discipline is not only good for maintaining good relationships with others, but also essential to raising a child with outstanding personal character. It helps in raising children that, when they grow up, will be less likely to engage in bad behaviors. Moreover, this person will be more likely to be well regarded by his/her peers and to receive positive assessments from supervisors and colleagues, thereby increasing his/her chances for career advancement.

Growing up in a working class Chinese family, I observed how my family and many other families put these principles to use in their parenting. As it turns out, families that stick to these principles tend to have well behaved and successful children whereas families that take a passive approach and are unwilling to discipline their children in regard to undesirable behaviors are likely to have bad behaved children.

From the example you can see that Confucianism-influenced Chinese parents start the moral education of their children at a young age. They are very sensitive to any signs of misbehavior in their children. They know in their hearts such strict discipline has invaluable long-term benefits. There is a Chinese saying: The big robber always starts with small stealing. By controlling misbehavior at the start when it is freshly rooted and relatively minor, it will prevent disastrous behavior from developing down the road. As you may recall from Chapter 2, Asian American students have the lowest rates in all behavioral measurements: use of alcohol, illicit drugs, teenage pregnancy, "carrying a weapon," and "engaged in a physical fight." These clearly correlate with Asian Americans having the lowest crime rates in the country.

3. Be willing to demand family members to "be better"
Having good discipline also helps the family to achieve its objectives. This also reflects in the willingness of Chinese American families to push their family members to work extra hard to achieve even greater

success. In almost all classic Confucian books, published family rules and norms, people are advocated to rise early, study and work hard, and bring success and honor to the family. Today, most Chinese Americans still uphold this good tradition. They are willing to demand family members to make an extra effort to achieve academic or career success. They often ask that family members "Be better," not just "Be yourself" as a popular value concept promoted in a lot of Hollywood movies.

As one approach for promoting individual equality and self-esteem, "Be yourself" has become a popular cultural concept in the US. It is true that a person should not pretend to be someone other than himself, which is the intention behind "Be yourself." However, too many people misinterpret these words to mean, "Keep the status quo" or "There's no need to improve yourself." Embracing such an attitude, some people do not care if their children have poor academic performance. But this is likely to lead to increased likelihood of unemployment or lower pay. Some people watch their weight spiral out of control without making a conscious effort to curb their appetite. But such behavior sooner or later will lead to diabetes and heart disease. Unfortunately, "Be yourself" gives a lot of people just the excuse they need to avoid doing the right thing.

It is worth mentioning that, over the last decades, with the increasing influence of modern psychology and the "self-esteem" movement, treating people gently and keeping others feeling good about themselves has become a prevailing behavior guideline. Gradually, it gets taken to an extreme. People are afraid of challenging others on undesirable behaviors. Teachers no longer criticize students for tardiness or demand sufficient academic performance. Parents become unwilling to discipline their children, avoiding any harsh words that may hurt their feelings, regardless of their merit. Many good traditions and worthwhile family disciplinary measures quietly recede under the influence of such doctrines. This directly leads to the failure of many families in today's American society.

As we have seen, Confucianism-influenced families take an aggressive approach to pursuing family success. They view discipline as a major component of love and strive for something that goes far beyond just keeping the family members happy. As "Tiger Mom" Amy Chua put it, "[Chinese parents] assume strength, not fragility."[20] They believe true love resides in a willingness to challenge family members to go above and beyond in order to achieve academic, career, and personal success. They believe individuals, adults and children alike, are much better equipped, psychologically and emotionally, to meet such challenges than some modern Western psychologists suggest. They set up ambitious goals and develop plans and schedules and implement them vigorously. They are not afraid of criticizing family members, urging them to do things that will benefit them today or in the long run. They believe the children and other family members have the psychological stamina to accept criticism and reasonable pressure to do better, and to go beyond their self-perceived comfort zone. With this kind of discipline, many Confucianism-influenced Chinese American families are able to thrive as families and as career professionals.

7.4 BALANCE CONFUCIAN FAMILY VALUES WITH WESTERN FAMILY VALUES

Family management is another area in which both Confucianism and Western values have their distinctive strengths. It is true the Western values of recognizing individuality and respect of equal rights are among the key success factors of modern civilization. It is very important to have individual rights and interests well presented in the family. In addition, encouragement of self-dependence and independent thinking is another strength of the Western family management approach.

However, if individualism is overemphasized it is possible the family members will have a reduced sense of devotion to the family. As a result, there is little to bond the family together. Without a strong sense of family responsibility, people may neglect the needs or interests of other family members, in particular the young and the elderly. If everybody becomes independent and has a strong ego, the family will be in constant dispute and possibly break up. In this case it will be even harder for the family to utilize its collective resources to achieve success for family members. Many families fail because of these reasons. This represents an undesirable extreme of the Western family management approach: being overly individualism-oriented.

On the contrary, if a traditional Confucian family management approach is implemented, the collective strengths of the family are better utilized. However, individual interests and rights tend to be underemphasized. The independent thinking and leadership abilities of non-leading family members are not properly encouraged. This represents an undesirable extreme of the Confucianism family management approach: being overly collectivism-oriented.

Can either of the two theories claim to be the correct one? Based on the social facts, the answer is no. This explains why, in recent centuries, Chinese families have gradually adopted many valuable concepts from Western family values. After observing some weaknesses of the Western family management approach, most Chinese American families choose to retain many effective Confucian family management values. In this way they reap the benefits of two important cultures. That is the approach Gary Locke's family, my family, and many other Asian American families have taken to achieve success.

Clearly, the optimal approach lies not at either extreme. But what is the proper combination of strengths from the two cultures? There is no set answer because it depends on the specific family situation— the structure, capabilities, and other factors of family members. Each person should find the solution that best fits his family's needs. Let's discuss three key topics: devotion to the family, spousal relationship, and parent-child relationship.

1. ***Devotion to the family:*** In terms of devotion to the family, there are three prime aspects: the normal responsibility of family members, in particular the parents; devotion to help those in need; and devotion to one family member's career success.

    • Normal responsibility of family members: It is in this area that Confucianism-influenced Chinese families show a lot of strength. The spouses emphasize family harmony, creating a stable family environment for each of the family members to pursue a career and/or a successful life. On top of that, the parents actively manage the family members' health, wellbeing, and moral behaviors. They also devote time and effort to the children's education, enabling them to have a great future. In the meantime, the children return the love to their parents. The siblings support one another and the family. If the parents have a good income, they support their children in their education. If not, they help them build a solid foundation in both academic and social skills. Clearly, while devoted to help the children to achieve their dreams, the parents should balance their needs for rest, recreation, and self-improvement. Such a balanced expression of love is shown to every family member.

- Devotion to help those in need: This is the case in which one family member is seriously ill, disabled, or infirm due to age. It requires extraordinary sacrifice that goes beyond normal family responsibilities. I have seen many American parents, influenced by Christianity or other moral values, devote a lot of time and effort to their disabled children or children suffering from autism, asthma, or other debilitating conditions. In this regard, both Western culture and Confucianism share the same value: Help those in need.

- Devotion to one family member's career success: This case, represented by the life stories of Michelle Kwan and Lang Lang, entails a family member having special talents and the potential to succeed in a big way. It calls for extraordinary sacrifice from the parents or other family members that exceeds normal family responsibilities. In this situation, a good question to ask is: Does the child have the potential to achieve a much bigger dream than you? In cases like Michelle Kwan and Lang Lang, the answer is yes. It was worthwhile for their parents to devote as much time, money, and effort as they did to support them in their journeys. The overall return on family investment was high.

If your child does not demonstrate this level of talent, it's better to let them pursue mainstream professions through a good education, such as engineer, lawyer, manager, or doctor. The pursuit of mainstream professions typically will not require such extraordinary sacrifice.

2. *Spousal relationship.* In this area, Confucianism finds its strength in family devotion and an emphasis on harmony, tolerance, and self-control. On the other side, Western culture finds its strength in respect for individual rights and interests, independence, and mutual respect. A good balance should have all these elements: The husband and wife treat and respect each other equally. Both are willing to devote reasonable effort to the other and to the children. Both have an appropriate level of tolerance for each other and self-control if a dispute arises. If the husband is more capable, he should take a leading role as the head of the household. If the wife is more capable, the roles should be reversed. It is very important to know that family happiness is the ends, equal rights is the means. The best family is typically managed by couples that can best utilize their strengths to work cooperatively. It is not necessarily best managed by couples that want to divide the rights equally regardless of their individual capabilities.

3. *Parent-child relationship.* This also calls for a balanced approach. On the one hand, we do not advocate the ancient Chinese way, an "authoritarian approach" in which the parents make all the decisions for the children. In this case, the child will run the risk of learning to be little more than a listener and follower. The development of their capacity for independent thinking, leadership, and reasonable skepticism will be impeded. On the other hand, we do not advocate the unbalanced practice adopted by some American families of letting children make their own decisions based purely on self-interest. If parents allow their children total freedom and are unwilling to exert an influence, the children will be incapable of managing either their academic performance or their behavior and will fail

to develop into disciplined people. This type of parenting is labeled "permissive" by sociologists. Taken to its extreme, this approach can lead to a "negligent" type of parenting, in which the children's economic, physical, academic, and ethical needs remain unaddressed by the parents. This type of parenting tends to produce children with a tendency to become criminals or who have other social problems. This is a totally unacceptable mode of parenting by either Confucian or Western standards. Many sociologists agree that "authoritative parenting," a combination of influential parenting and encouragement of children's independent thinking, is one of the best parenting approaches. In this approach, parents need to look out for their children's long-term development and bring broad knowledge and experienced decision-making skills to the task of raising the children. The parents set up and implement proper rules for the children to follow. Very importantly, they explain the purpose and principles behind these rules. With love and care, the children are raised to appreciate both discipline and an independent way of thinking. Again, this is not a fixed, cookie-cutter approach that should be applied to every child at any age group. Generally speaking, the degree of parental influence should be at an inverse relationship with the children's age and ability. When the children are young or less capable, more parental influence is needed and it should be more on the authoritarian side. When the children reach high school or college age, less parental influence is needed. The parents need to lean toward a more democratic style of decision making. The faster the child develops the knowledge and discipline, the sooner the parents should encourage their participation in the decision making.

Again, family management is like many other things, and adopting wisdom from multiple cultures is typically better than drawing exclusively from only one.

Chapter 8

FIFTH VALUE: *ZE-YOU* (择友)

"Developing Desirable Friendships"—Confucian Value of Developing Friendships That Benefit Your Life

8.1 THE IMPORTANCE OF FRIENDSHIP AND HAVING THE RIGHT FRIENDS

At the end of 2010, Mark Zuckerberg was selected as the Person of the Year by *Time Magazine* for having founded Facebook.com, the most popular social networking website in history, which had attracted 550 million memberships worldwide by 2010.[1] This dramatically underscores the importance of friendship in modern society.

There are many distinctive advantages of a successful friendship.

First, it extends your circle of emotional, social, and other support beyond just family members. Friends can provide you with much needed help, trust, and comfort in your time of need. Under normal conditions, friends give each other a hand, offer advice, and share life experiences. Friendship gives people a sense of belonging and being grounded. In emergency situations, such as a hurricane or family mishap, friends offer each other invaluable support in overcoming life's obstacles.

Second, by cultivating friendships you expose yourself to different perspectives, which in turn broadens your knowledge base and enhances your living skills. In particular, when your friends share with you their experiences, you have instant access to valuable information you otherwise would not have had or would have gained at the expense of a considerable time investment and/or lessons learned. Imagine entering a new company or moving into a new neighborhood… It will take much longer for you to become familiar with the new environment if there are no friends to show you around, or share with you their experience.

Third, it allows you to access more social resources and expand your social activity arena. This is particularly true if you have successful friends. By networking with them, you may access their friends, who may be able to refer you to a job prospect or a good mentor who can help you or your children. In today's America, networking and personal referral are among the most effective ways to find good jobs. Similarly, they are among the most effective ways to find excellent teachers/ coaches for your children or a top-notch doctor.

Fourth, friendship is good for your health. A friend will let you know when s/he notices an unhealthy trend or development in your health. Good friends are a source of comfort and help each other solve problems when difficulties present themselves. Studies have shown that all of these factors contribute to good health.

According to a 2006 study, since 1985 there has been an unhealthy trend in the US of having fewer close friendships. It was reported that 25% of Americans have no close friends and the average number of total close friends has dropped from four to two. One of the consequences of such a decline in close friendships is an increasing dependence on the family. Americans' dependence on partners or spouses went up from 5% to 9%, and reliance on family as a safety net went from 57% in 1985 to 80% in 2006. Here we clearly see the disadvantages of not having successful friendships.[2]

Having friendships with bad people is another serious problem for many families and society as a whole. Bad friends create bad influences and facilitate crimes. According to criminal psychology, forming a gang (criminal group) is likely to increase the probability of a crime occurring. First, criminals may provide assistance to one another. With support, many impossible crimes become possible. More importantly, "peer encouragement" plays an important role in initiating crimes. If a person intends to commit a crime alone, he may rethink the consequences of the crime before he takes action. If two or more people act together, the sense of bravery is inflated, increasing the likelihood that one of them will initiate the crime without thinking through the consequences. Similarly, making friends with undesirable people exposes you and your family to undesirable influences. Many bad behaviors such as drug abuse and gambling are typically introduced by bad friends.

8.2 CONFUCIAN VALUE OF *ZE-YOU* (择友)— DEVELOPING DESIRABLE FRIENDSHIPS

As a great mind addressing social issues, Confucius recognized friendship as one of the most important relationships in human society. In the "Ten Human Duties" defined in the Confucian classic, the *Book of Rites* (礼记), friendship is addressed in #7 and #8, following the first six human duties, which address family relationships.[3]

> (7) *Peng-xin* (朋信): Friends should treat each other with trust.
> (8) *You-yi* (友义): Friends should help each other for the right cause.

Including these two duties, Confucius and his followers have laid out many insightful guidelines in this important area. They address several key aspects of friendship:

1. Differentiate good friends from bad

Confucius did not think all friends were equally beneficial to your life. Some are good friends, which can benefit you, and some are bad friends, which can do you harm. He said, "There are three types of beneficial friends and three types of detrimental friends. Beneficial friends are those who are frank towards friends, those who are trustworthy, and who have broad experiences and viewpoints. Detrimental friends are those who are biased, those who use flattery, and those who are full of bragging and misleading words (益者三友，损者三友。友直，友谅，友多闻，益矣。友便辟，友善柔，友便佞，损矣)."[4]

Xun Zi (荀子), another key Confucian scholar, had a similar view. He said, "A person who can criticize me correctly is my teacher; A person who praises me correctly is my friend; A person who flatters me is just like a thief (非我而当者，吾师也；是我而当者，吾友也；谄谀我者，吾贼也)."[5]

Mencius added further criteria with regard to making friends. He said, "One cannot make good conversation with a person with a bad temper. One cannot collaborate with a person who is a self-defeatist (自暴者不可与有言也，自弃者不可与有为也)."[6] These guidelines retain their value, despite the fact they were written more than 2,500 years ago.

2. Select the right friends

Recognizing the benefits of having good friends and the drawbacks of having bad friends, Confucianism advocates strongly for appropriate friend selection. Xun Zi (荀子) said, "One should select nice people as friends. One should be prudent when selecting friends because friends form the foundation for one's moral development (取友善人，不可不慎。是德之基也。)."[7]

How do you select the right friends? After all, people don't come with a label stating they are a good person or a bad person. As early as 2,500 years ago, Confucius had identified such challenges and provided his advice: "Listen to what he says, observe how he acts, and understand his purpose. How can't you have a good assessment of this person (视其所以，观其所由，察其所安。人焉廋哉？)?"[8] It is very important to watch how one acts, and comprehend his purpose, and not be misled by his words. Today, it is still a valid process in evaluating a person, in particular a friend.

In addition to selecting friends with good moral characteristics, Confucianism also suggests selecting friends with whom you share common interests. Confucius said, "If there is no common interest, the two should not cooperate together (道不同，不相为谋)."[9] Having friends with common interests will lead to more shared values and mutual benefits than if there are no interests in common.

3. Select the right neighborhood to live in

The founders of Confucianism looked not only at the issue of making individual friends, but at the neighborhood a person lives in as well. You can select the people you wish to make your friends and visit each other at your and their convenience. However, you will see your neighbors every day after you select the neighborhood to live in. More importantly, your children are likely to play with your neighbors' children on a daily basis. As a result, Confucianism also advocates that one should be prudent in selecting the neighborhood where you will live. Confucius stated, "It is beneficial to live with people of high moral values. If you do not live with such people, how can you say that you are wise (里仁为美。择不处仁，焉得知?)?"[10] Xun Zi also said, "When a gentleman selects a place to live, he must select a good community. When a gentleman travels, he must visit people with knowledge and good moral values. In this way, he can avoid bad influence and stay close to rightful influences (君子居必择乡，游必就士，所以防邪僻而近中正也)."[11]

"Three Word Chant" told the story of how Mencius' mother selected their homes in order to raise Mencius surrounded by desirable influences when Mencius was young. As a widow raising her son by herself, she had a big dream: She wanted to raise Mencius to become a well-educated scholar. At first, they lived in a community where most people engaged in funeral ceremonies. Influenced by his neighbors, the child Mencius developed an interest in learning how to play the musical instruments for the funerals. That disappointed Mencius' mother because the influence on Mencius was not what she wanted. As a result, she moved the family to another neighborhood. As it turned out, many ironsmiths and small business vendors lived in this new neighborhood. They engaged daily in business bargains. Very soon, Mencius developed an interest in selling and bargaining. Again, this was not in line with the expectations of Mencius' mother. She moved again, finally settling down in a house beside a school. This time, things turned out as Mencius' mother hoped. Influenced by his neighbors, Mencius developed a strong interest in learning, eventually becoming the second most influential scholar of Confucianism.[12]

4. Develop and maintain successful friendships

Confucian values related to developing and maintaining friendship have two important layers. The first layer consists of the approaches Confucianism advocates governing how people should treat each other in general. As early as 2,500 years ago, when most of the world was dominated by brutal slavery systems, Confucius was advocating that people should treat one another in a humane and respectful way, give to the needy, and be lenient with others. These general principles are preconditions for developing and maintaining successful relationships. They are discussed in the first three points below. As friendship runs deeper than typical interpersonal relationships, Confucius added three specific guiding principles as follows that will greatly help you in building successful friendships. They will be discussed in #4 through #6 of the following section.

1) *Treat other people humanely*

Treating people in a humane way, with high moral standards (仁, pronounced as *ren*), is one of the core values of Confucianism. As introduced in Chapter 3, Confucius and Mencius set up many good principles in this area:

- "A humane person loves other people. A person with good manners respects other people. A person who loves other people will always be loved. A person who respects other people will always be respected (仁者爱人，有礼者敬人。爱人者，人恒爱之。敬人者，人恒敬之)."—Mencius[13]

- The standard to treat other people should be how you expect other people to treat you. "What you do not want done to yourself, do not do to others (己所不欲，勿施与人)."—Confucius[14]
- "A gentleman should do things to help others to achieve happy results, should not undermine others' happiness (君子成人之美，不成人之恶)."—Confucius[15]

What Confucianism advocates are that people should have good intentions and treat one another nicely. They should not do anything to harm others. Clearly, these are essential behavior guidelines for dealing with other people, including making friends.

2) Help those who are in great need

Another good illustration of the great humanity advocated by Confucianism is in the area of helping others. Confucius said, "A gentleman should help those who are in great need, not the ones who are already rich (君子周急而不济富)."[16] Helping the needy is one of most humane ways to behave in a society. It is a smart way to make friends because helping the needy will create greater gratitude and value than enhancing someone who is already rich. For example, let's say you want to give away $100. If you give it to an orphan who is starving, it may save his life. If you give it to a rich person, it will barely impact his life. Giving to the needy is a humane approach that reflects the donor's big heart, as opposed to snobbish people who are primarily interested in pleasing the rich and the powerful. In the thousands of years since Confucius said it, Chinese society has converted it into a popular phrase: "A person should prefer sending coal to others in a snowy cold winter [to keep them warm] to adding one more flower to a beautifully made brocade (宁可雪中送炭，不可锦上添花)." This has become a well-known guideline for most Chinese to deal with interpersonal relationships. It also converges with the Christian values of helping the poor and supporting charities, which are cherished by American society.

3) Be strict with oneself and lenient toward others

In addition to treating other people with good intentions and kindness, Confucianism recognizes the issue of dispute resolution. In case two people are involved in some sort of disagreement, how should they behave? To address this problem, Confucianism imposes a very high moral standard: Be strict with oneself and lenient toward others (严以律己、宽以待人) As mentioned in chapter 7, Confucius said, "If you are willing to blame yourself more than others [when a dispute arises], you will avoid being hated by others (躬自厚而薄责于人，则远怨矣)."[17] By being willing to take one step back, you eliminate a potential source of animosity, and possibly generate gratitude from others. If one or both parties adopt this attitude, the dispute can be settled with ease. This attitude is also a valuable guideline in dealing with potential disputes between friends.

4) Treat friends with trust

In addition to the above guidelines on how to treat personal relationships, Confucianism advocates higher standards for how to treat friendship. The first is trust. As written in #7 of the "Ten Human Duties" *Peng-Xin* (朋信), Confucianism regards mutual trust as the foundation of friendship. With trust, friends can share what is really on their minds, be it hardship or joy. Without trust, friends cannot depend on each other and no close friendship can be formed.

5) Give friends rightful help

The key benefit of having a friendship is to provide help to each other. In #8 of the "Ten Human Duties" *You-Yi* (友义), Confucianism advocates friends should help each other for the right cause. Here, Confucianism emphasizes both "help" and "for the right cause." In his view, a person is obligated to help a friend if he is in need of help for the right cause. It also implies that a person should not help a friend if the cause is not right. When friends help each other, the friendship bond is strengthened. When the help is not for the right cause, a person will step into troubled water for a friend's wrong cause. This is what friends should rightly expect from each other and a key guideline for developing and maintaining a good friendship.

6) Be prudent about your communication

To maintain friendships, one needs to pay attention to communication with friends. There is a Chinese saying: "Diseases are typically brought in by mouth; Disasters are typically brought about through the mouth (病从口入；祸从口出)." This clearly underscores the importance of communication skills. If the wrong words are used to communicate to the right person, or right words are used to communicate to the wrong person, it can create misunderstandings or even disasters. Confucius stated, "If you do not tell your friend something he should know, you may lose a friend. If you tell a friend something you should not tell him, you may have a miscommunication. A wise person should not lose a friend or mis-communicate (可与言而不与之言，失人;不可与言而与言，失言。知者不失人，亦不失言。)."[18] Confucius advises we be prudent about our communication: Say the right thing to the right person. In this way, prudent communication enhances friendship and reduces misunderstanding between friends. In this way friendship can last.

The above Confucian principles on friendship entail the fifth Chinese secret for success: Developing desirable friendships that benefit your work and your life. In the following section I will explain how these good principles are applied in Chinese society.

8.3 HOW THE CHINESE APPLY CONFUCIAN PRINCIPLES IN DEVELOPING BENEFICIAL AND LONG-LASTING FRIENDSHIPS

Like most other societies, Chinese society regards friendship as one of the most important social relationships. A well-known Chinese phrase points to a simple principle: "When you are young at home, you depend on your parents; After you leave home, you depend on your friends (在家靠父母；出门靠朋友)." Like other aspects of Chinese society, the values regarding friendship are deeply influenced by Confucianism. Over the last two thousand years, Chinese people have been following these valuable guidelines and in some areas even further developed a lot of wisdom and good practices. Following are a few good practices used by Confucianism influenced Chinese families, including Chinese Americans.

#1 Know How to Distinguish Friends

Starting with Confucius, Chinese people have recognized the importance of the influence of friends. A very famous Chinese phrase goes: "One who stays near vermilion gets stained red, and one who stays near ink gets stained black (近朱者赤，近墨者黑)." This is quite similar to an English phrase: "One takes the behavior of one's company." In order to help people distinguish between good and bad friendships, over the last two thousand years, Chinese people have summarized many experiences regarding friendship and categorized. them by type. The most common are as follows:

1. *Gangster friends*, also called "friends between foxes and wild dogs (*hu-peng-gou-you*, 狐朋狗友)" literally in Chinese. These include criminals or people who engage in bad behavior. They engage in wrong causes. Clearly, a friendship with this type of person are what every good person wants to avoid.

2. *Party-only friends*, also called "beer and beef friends (*jiu-rou-peng-you*, 酒肉朋友)" literally in Chinese. These include people who are chiefly interested in partying and entertaining. When one of them has money to spend, they come around wanting to eat and drink and have fun. However, when you need help they do not come through for you as a true friend would. This is another type of friend that wise people try to avoid.

3. *Regular friends*, which are called *fan-fan-zhi-jiao* (泛泛之交) in Chinese. They treat each other nicely and friendly. They provide help to each other if it does not involve too much money, time, or effort. They share information about life, but not a lot of personal secrets.

4. *Close friends*, which are called *mo-ni-zhi-jiao* or *zhi-jiao* (莫逆之交 or 至交) in Chinese. They trust each other and are

willing to provide help beyond regular friendship. They share personal secrets and trade advice to help each other deal with many personal issues. One is willing to devote significant time, money, or effort to help the other for the right cause. They treat each other like brothers or sisters. This is the type of friendship people want to have.

5. *Tested friends,* which are called *huan-nan-zhi-jiao* (患难之交) in Chinese. It describes a friendship that was formed during a hardship in which two people provided essential help to each other. It is regarded as a proven and trusted friendship people should treasure. This typically develops into a close friendship.

6. *Cross-generational friends,* which are called *wang-nian-zhi-jiao* (忘年之交) in Chinese. It describes a friendship formed between people who belong to different generations. It is typically formed based on shared interests or assistance rendered. Typically, the senior provides the junior with wisdom and guidance, while the junior provides the senior with help in the areas in which the youth can do better, from moving heavy things to surfing the Internet.

Obviously, people should avoid the first two types of friendship and develop friendships with desirable people. In order to assess a person's characteristics, Confucius suggests we listen to what a person says, observe how he acts, and comprehend his purpose. Usually it is very difficult to gauge one's true character overnight. As a result, some wise Chinese scholars suggest: A person's true heart will be revealed over the time (事久见人心). It takes time to evaluate a friend, to understand his moral value before you can trust or depend on him/her fully.

#2 Always Avoid Bad or Undesirable Friends
It is not necessarily true that if you are friends with a bad or undesirable person you will have an unsuccessful life. But the likelihood of it happening will be much higher if you choose to do so. Confucianism advocates a person should select friends wisely, in

order to avoid detrimental risk and achieve a successful life. Many Confucianism-influenced Chinese American families take this conservative approach to minimize family risks.

There are two types of people you should not make friends with. The first is people who behave badly. They engage in violence, drug trafficking, gang activities, and other illegal behaviors. They are not the friends you want to make unless you want to risk being influenced by their behavior.

The second type is people with undesirable behaviors. The three types identified by Confucius are not the sort of people you want to pick as friends: those who are biased, those who use flattery, and those who brag a lot and use misleading words. In addition, in Chinese society, people who exhibit detrimental behavior with their families are not desirable as friends. They include people who

- are addicted to drugs, gambling;
- exhibit violent behavior and extremely bad manners in treating people;
- are too selfish or too greedy;
- are compulsive and overindulgent in spending or personal recreation;
- are interested only in partying and not willing to help their friends—"beer and beef friends."

Here I'd like to point out that in discussing evaluating people, selecting the "right" people as your friends, some may have the mistaken impression that we are talking about a sort of discrimination. Clearly, everyone should fully recognize the equal rights of all people, even those who have bad or undesirable behaviors. However, taking care to select the right friends is a basic freedom of each individual. Any person deserves the right to evaluate other people based on whichever set of criteria they choose to employ. Logically, if people make fewer friends with individuals who have bad or undesirable behavior, such behavior will be discouraged in their own lives.

#3 Ensure Your Children Make
Well Behaved and Progressive Friends

The children are always the focus of most Chinese families. This is also true with regard to friendship. Children have two features that distinguish them from adults. The first is they are very curious about the world they grow up in. They want to learn a lot of stuff. The second is that children are not as knowledgeable as adults and have little ability to differentiate between good people and bad people. These two factors make children extremely vulnerable to bad influences. In today's American society, children face ready exposure to an array of bad influences, including drug abuse, gang activity, and other risky behaviors.

Because of this, many responsible American parents enroll their children in various after-school programs in order to keep their children occupied and away from bad influences. In addition to engaging children in after-school activities, Confucianism-influenced Chinese American families typically keep a close eye on the friends their children make. If there is a sign they are associating with undesirable people, the parents will immediately step in and ask their children to end the relationship. This is key to controlling the potential downside of any high-risk friendships.

At the same time, Confucianism-influenced Chinese families make an effort to maximize the upside of their children's beneficial friendships. According to the *Book of Rites*, when students learn together, they broaden their knowledge by sharing and encourage learning from one another (大学之法…相观而善之谓摩).[19] By recognizing the significant influence of friends, many Chinese American families encourage their children to play with kids who have good behaviors, are interested in learning, and are ambitious. This creates worthwhile peer influence and peer competition that will encourage their children to make progress. On the contrary, party girls and party boys are typically not welcomed by Chinese parents.

Group learning is especially valuable when involved in a dedicated or specialized mission such as learning a foreign language or preparing for a science or mathematics competition. While preparing for graduate study in the US, I attended a reputable training school in Beijing. In this school, every student studied very hard to learn English. We discussed how to solve test problems. We also went to places we called "English Corners," where many English learners got together in the evening to practice speaking English. Without such effective group learning, it would have taken a much longer time for me to improve my English and be able to be accepted by an American graduate school. Many readers may not know that in most American cities you will find Chinese schools operated by Chinese parents on a volunteer basis. Since most American public schools do not offer Chinese language education, these parents use their spare time to organize such schools so their children can learn Chinese effectively, in a group learning environment.

#4 Find Mentors Whose Advice and Influence Can Benefit Your Career and Your Life

When a person starts out in his/her career, s/he does not have a lot of experience. Many challenges lay ahead for this person: How to handle organizational relationships? How to become quickly familiar with the technology, the product, and/or the market your company is involved in? How to gain more professional skills? With an experienced mentor who can navigate this young employee through, his/her career development will be accelerated.

A similar principle also applies to life. Parents typically play the role of mentor. However, if you move to another place where your parents' knowledge is limited, or if your parents do not have a successful life, you will find a mentor other than your parents is very valuable.

In Chinese society, the mentor concept started when Confucius and other scholars began to disseminate their teachings more than 2,500 years ago. A teacher typically has many students or disciples. The teacher plays the role of mentor, passing on his/her knowledge and advice on career and life and helping the disciple to find a good job. In return, the disciple pays great respect to the teacher, assisting the teacher and his/her family. In ancient times before machinery was widely available, the young disciples provided physical help to the older teacher, who typically was not as physically strong as farmers or people in other labor-intensive professions. They helped the teacher's family by carrying heavy items and sometimes doing chores. In case a family member of the teacher was sick, the students would provide any needed help.

This tradition continues in Chinese society today. A good mentor is typically called "a fine mentor and beneficial friend (良师益友)" by his disciples or other people of younger generations. Many Chinese people, including myself, develop friendships with such mentors for guidance and help in career and life development.

Over a professional career spanning more than twenty years, I have benefited from the kindness and professional integrity of many mentors. I grew up in a working class family in Kunming, Yunnan Province. As my hometown was not economically advanced, in order to pursue a big dream, I chose to develop my career in Beijing and later in the US, two unfamiliar places that were filled with challenges. Fortunately, I was able to get help from many mentors at almost every important step in my career development. In Beijing, one mentor helped me land a good job, doing industrial strategy development. Another mentor helped me to develop many professional skills and assisted me in writing the industrial strategy book I published. Other mentors wrote recommendations to accompany my applications to American graduate schools. In the US, kind graduate school professors offered me graduate assistantships, and helped me and my wife survive the initial years of culture shock and economic difficulties in the US. Once I was employed, another mentor guided my career development in the US and sponsored my path toward US citizenship. Without such help, I, a poor child from Kunming, would never have attained the good life in the US I have today.

People may ask, how do you develop such good relationships with so many nice mentors? My experience has taught me: Find the mentors who have good hearts and high professional integrity. Treat them with kindness, respect, and politeness as Confucius advises. Also work hard, apply your talents, and generate good results for the school where you study or the company you work for. It is the way you treat friends and your work that builds trust with your mentors.

After a person gains experience and influence, s/he is likely to find that young people will start asking him/her for advice and help. Most likely, this person will be happy to become a mentor to the younger generation. The mentor-disciple relationship continues generation by generation among many Chinese. History has proven that having a mentor is very beneficial to the development of young people. Today, many American corporations also initiate mentor programs to accelerate the learning and career development of young employees.

#5 Develop Close Friends Who Can Be Trusted and Depended On

Having one or more trusted and dependable friends is extremely helpful in your life and for your career. If you live by yourself, you depend primarily on your personal knowledge and skills to make a living. If you form a family, your knowledge base and support are doubled or tripled because all family members share the knowledge and provide help to one another. The same is true when you develop trusted and dependable friends. In Chinese culture, close friends are viewed as an extension of your family. They have a few basic qualities:

1. Close friends keep each other's best interest in mind when making relevant decisions; this is called *wei-peng-you-zhuo-xiang* (为朋友着想) in Chinese.
2. Close friends treat each other with trust and integrity, which in Confucianism is referred to as *peng-xin* (朋信).
3. Close friends are willing to help each other with a significant time, effort, or financial commitment for the right cause; this is called *you-yi* (友义) in Confucianism.
4. Close friends will be straightforward in pointing out each other's strengths and weaknesses, and help each other to improve; this is called *you-zhi* (友直) in Confucianism.

In Western society, where individual privacy and self-esteem are highly valued, it may be difficult to point out weaknesses in a friend.

If one wants to make improvements in one's career or life, however, one should encourage more open and straightforward communication between close friends so both sides will benefit from criticism/advice, as long as it is offered honestly and with good intentions.

Developing a close friendship, good moral values, and good behaviors are musts. In addition, according to Confucius, it is preferred to pick as friends those people who have similar career goals and shared interests. This is called *zhi-tong-dao-he* (志同道合) in Chinese. If two people are at different places in their professional lives they will have different attitudes toward life and career. One friend might be very ambitious, hard working, and anxious to improve his career whereas the other lacks ambition and just wants to enjoy life. In this case, there is little chance they will become close friends. Similarly, shared interests stimulate a lot of common discussion, joint projects, and shared actions so a strong friendship can develop. Very often, high school and college classmates easily form a close relationship for this very reason. Such was the case with Jerry Yang and David Filo. They met at Stanford in 1989. They went to Japan together. In 1995, building on their shared interests and determination, they jointly founded Yahoo.[20]

#6 Extend Your Circle of Friends to Include Many of Your Acquaintances

As we all know, developing a close friendship requires high levels of trust and commitment between two people. Thanks to inventions such as Facebook and Twitter, communication between friends has been made much more efficient. The American lifestyle can be pretty hectic, however, demanding of your time, and the chances for you to make a lot of close friends in your lifetime are limited. In addition, you do not want to share your personal secrets with too many people. To make your life successful and pleasant, you should extend your circle of friends to include many of your acquaintances. These may include your neighbors, colleagues, and people with whom you interface regularly. Some of them may eventually become your close friends. However, you should treat a lot of them as *regular friends*. We call it *fan-fan-zhi-jiao* (泛泛之交) in Chinese. In this way, you will have a large circle of friends in which things are kept on a nice, friendly basis. Such friends provide help to each other to a reasonable degree. They share good information about work, about life, and about the community in which they live together.

In fact, Western society, including the US, has done a marvelous job in terms of treating people nicely and extending friendships to include many others. While living in the US or traveling in other Western countries, I have found people are eager to provide help if asked, such as giving directions, referring you to good doctors or restaurants, and being forthcoming with advice. They are willing to provide kind help to others without any expectation of getting something in return. Personal kindness and trust prevail in these societies, where Confucian and Western values clearly converge.

Influenced by both Confucian and Western values, many Chinese Americans make a conscious effort to cultivate friendships. For example, Chinese students attending American colleges often form student associations. In many American cities, Chinese Americans likewise bond together through various organizations. In this way, they make friends, share useful information, and provide help to one another. This is especially helpful for Chinese newcomers who have recently arrived in America. These people typically experience major culture shock because the U.S. living and working environments are so different from what they were familiar with in China. By networking with established immigrants, they can settle down in their lives much faster and easier.

It is worth pointing out that due to the language barrier and the influence of the traditional Chinese value of modesty, some first generation immigrants from China are not aggressive enough in building their friend network beyond other ethnic Chinese. In recent decades, more and more Chinese immigrants have been able to take a more open and aggressive approach, successfully building relationships across cultural barriers that help them advance their careers and lives significantly.

#7 Choose Your Neighborhood Wisely

A neighborhood is a collection of landscapes, physical facilities such as stores, schools, and churches, and importantly, individuals. Their behavior will have an impact on your life. In particular, as your children are likely to play with your neighbors' children, the families in the neighborhood will have a significant impact on your children's lives—their safety, their behavior development, and their school performance.

As an ethnic group with a marked devotion to the development of the next generation, most Chinese American families are very selective when it comes to choosing a neighborhood because this decision can largely shape their children's education and character development. The story regarding how Mencius' mother selected her neighborhood is well known among Chinese families. Almost every Chinese family I know always tries their best to choose a house in a neighborhood that has A-rated elementary, middle, and high schools. That is typically the first priority when selecting a neighborhood. Along with that, the safety of the neighborhood, residential structure, and proximity to the workplace are important criteria for selecting a neighborhood.

Many non-Chinese Americans likewise make a significant effort to select a neighborhood with good schools and other promising conditions. What distinguishes Confucianism-influenced Chinese Americans is their willingness to sacrifice other criteria—or money earmarked for other uses—in order to buy a house in a good school district. The house can be smaller, the driving distance can be longer, the mortgage payment can be higher, as long as their home is located in a good school district and in a neighborhood with nice people they can be friends with. This practice is also shared by many other Asian Americans.

Although it means a higher mortgage, selecting a nice neighborhood clearly pays off for most Chinese or non-Chinese Americans. In such neighborhoods, crime activity is very low or nonexistent, risky behaviors such as drug abuse are quite rare, neighbors have a good education and treat one another nicely, and very importantly, kids are willing to learn and behave. Once the family has selected a good external environment they can focus on their career, their life, and how to raise the children successfully.

#8 Treat Your Friends with Trust, Respect, Lenience, and Consideration

Knowing what kind of friends one should make and what kind of neighborhood one should choose is only the first step in terms of forming successful friendships with your friends and neighbors. It takes a good heart, good words, and more importantly, good actions to receive the same from someone else. This is the essence of forming and maintaining good relationships. This is called "using a good heart to exchange for another good heart (以心换心)" in Chinese.

Knowingly or unknowingly, many Chinese Americans benefit from Confucian teaching with regard to how to treat other people and friends in a moral way. Many Confucian values in this area have become part of daily language in Chinese culture. For example, when dealing with interpersonal relationships, many Confucianism-influenced Chinese frequently rely on an idiom that calls for them to "think on someone [else]'s behalf (将心比己)." It requires one to have a deep comprehension of the other party's concern and interests. This is a reflection of Confucius' famous words: "What you do not want done to yourself, do not do to others (己所不欲，勿施与人)."

To recapture an earlier discussion, the following Confucian values are still widely used by many Chinese Americans when dealing with friendship:

1) Treat other people humanely, including
   - Have good intentions and love for other people (仁者爱人)
   - Give proper respect to other people (有礼者敬人)
   - Try to understand someone's situation before you take actions that may have an impact on this person (将心比己)
   - Help others to achieve happy results (成人之美).

2) Help those who are in great need, not those who are already rich (君子周急而不济富).

3) Be strict with oneself and lenient toward others (严以律己、宽以待人).

4) Treat friends with trust (朋信).

5) Give friends rightful help (友义).

6) Be prudent about your communication; use the right words with the right person (知者不失人，亦不失言).

Today, such pearls of wisdom still reap benefits for many Chinese communities, including many Chinese Americans, helping to guide them in developing and maintaining friendships with desirable people. The more these guidelines are heeded, the more success people can achieve in enriching their lives.

ABOUT THE AUTHOR

 **YuKong Zhao is the** Director of China Business Development of Siemens Energy Inc. He grew up in a Confucianism-influenced family in China and emigrated to the US in 1992. He is an expert in China strategies and has published an industrial strategy book in China. He was interviewed by Wen Jiabao in 2001, then the Deputy Premier of China, and featured by the Chinese Central Radio Station in 2004 as a successful overseas Chinese. His professional and personal activities have provided him with great insight into successful elements of Chinese and American cultural values. He lives with his wife and two high-achieving, well-rounded school-age children in Orlando, Florida.

ACKNOWLEDGEMENTS

FIRST, I WANT TO express my deepest love and thanks to my family, who inspired me to learn and apply our valuable cultural heritage in the form of inspiring Confucian values:

My grandfather, who has provided me with vital help during critical times in my life. When I was very young, he told me heroic stories of ancient China that inspired me to *li-zhi*, to have a big dream for my life. When I was in elementary school, he taught me "Three Word Chant," the secular Bible of Confucianism, in a positive way at a time that the Maoist government was attacking Confucianism. Even with very weak eyesight, he still took care of me, cooked for me every day during my middle and high school years. Without it, I would not have had the chance to go to one of the best universities in China and to come to the US later on.

My mother, who gave me the greatest love a mother can give and provided care to me until she was unable to. Her positivism, life wisdom, and way of caring for friends and relatives have set up a role model for me and shaped my character. When my father was persecuted during the Cultural Revolution, she provided love and crucial protection to my family and many relatives. Unfortunately, she passed away too early to enjoy the prosperous life my generation experienced after Deng Xiaoping's economic reform.

My father, who always loved me and worked diligently to support the family despite extraordinary difficulties he suffered during the turmoil of modern China. He taught me a true sense of responsibility, resilience, and a "can do" attitude, which benefited my life beyond measure.

My lovely and loving wife, Wenlan Li, who is a wonderful woman and a great mother to my children. Her love and devotion to me and our family have been essential in every achievement we've made and the many happy and memorable moments of our life together as a family. Her comments and support during the writing of this book have been invaluable.

My proud children, Hubert and Selena, who give us the greatest joy and sense of happiness as parents. They were a strong motivation for me to write this book, in order to let them know about and sustain the great cultural heritage that is ours.

In addition, I'd like to expresses my thanks to my great friends, who provided insights and comments on my book: my best neighbor William Dorsey, my best real estate agent Wendy and her husband Andrew Patton, my former graduate study advisor Ted Koebel, and my former project supervisor Marilyn Cavel at Virginia Tech. I also want to thank my artist friend, Shelley Overton, whose talent has helped in improving my book cover design significantly.

In particular, I'd like to express my special thanks to my editor, Karl Monger. In spite of many family difficulties, he expended great energy on my manuscript and dramatically improved its English. Without Karl's command of the language, it would be very difficult for me to communicate these great Chinese wisdoms effectively to an American audience.

I also want to thank those who provided advice, suggestions, and referrals along my journey to having this book published. They include:

Simon Bailey, Janet Goldstein, Lloyd Lofthouse, Michael Ebeling, and C.S. Kiang.

Finally, I want to express my thanks to my publisher Morgan James Publishing and its staff. Dave Sauer patiently addressed my many questions, Jim Howard and Lyza Poulin assisted in the publishing process, and David Hancock, Rick Frishman and Bethany Marshall provided me with great advice on the marketing side of the journey.

NOTES

INTRODUCTION

1. "China GDP Growth," *Index Mundi,* http://www.indexmundi.com/china/gdp_real_growth_rate.html (accessed April 30, 2011).

2. United States Department of Commerce, "Gross Domestic Product, Percent Change From Preceding Period," Bureau of Economic Analysis, http://www.bea.gov/national/index.htm#gdp (accessed April 30, 2011).

3. Kamal Ahmed, "Jim O'Neill: China Could Overtake US Economy by 2027," *Telegraph,* November 19, 2011.

4. Mary Bruce, "China Debuts at Top of International Education Rankings," ABC News, December 7, 2011.

5. Herman Kahn, "The Confucian Ethic and Economic Growth," in *World Economic Development: 1979 and Beyond* (Westview, 1979), 121–123.

6. Roderick MacFarquar, "The Post-Confucian Challenge," *The Economist,* February 9, 1980: 67–72.

7. Pew Research Center, "The Rise of Asian Americans," June 19, 2012, 1.

8. United States Department of Commerce, "Income, Poverty, and Health Insurance Coverage in the United States: 2009," US Census Bureau Current Population Reports, September 2010.

9. Pew Research Center, "The Rise of Asian Americans," 2, 37.

10. Catherine Rampell, "College Enrollment Rate at Record High," *The New York Times,* April 28, 2010.

11. Timothy Egan, "Asian-Americans Challenge Ideas of Race in US Universities," *International Herald Tribune,* January 7, 2007.

12. Please see detailed data and sources in chapter 2, section 2.2.

13. Palash R. Ghosh, "Asian-Americans Endure Well During Recession, But 'Model Minority' Theory Has Some Holes in It," *International Business Times,* July 29, 2010.

14. "Leibniz on China, from the Preface to the Novissima Sinica (1697/1699)," http://east_west_dialogue.tripod.com/id12.html (accessed April 12, 2011).

15. Confucius et al., *Four Books & Five Classics,* ed. Zefei Li (Shenyang: Wanjuan Publishing House 2009), 66.

CHAPTER 1: CHALLENGING TIMES ARE AHEAD

1. Anthony Gregory, "What Price War: Afghanistan, Iraq, and the Costs of Conflict," The Independent Institute, June 2011, 9.

2. "Crude Oil Price History," http://www.nyse.tv/crude-oil-price-history. htm (accessed March 12, 2011).

3. United States Department of Labor, Bureau of Labor Statistics, "Databases, Tables, and Calculators by Subject," http://data.bls.gov/ cgi-bin/surveymost (accessed March 15, 2011).

4. United States Bureau of Labor Statistics, "The 2010 Census: The Employment Impact of Counting the Nation," *Monthly Labor Review,* March 2011, 33.

5. RealtyTrac Staff, "Record 2.9 Million US Properties Receive Foreclosure Filings in 2010 Despite 30-Month Low in December," January 13, 2011, http://www.realtytrac.com/content/foreclosure-market-report/record-29-million-us-properties-receive-foreclosure-filings-in-2010-despite-30-month-low-in-december-6309.

6. George Howell and Kyle Almond, "Many American Families Running on Financial Fumes," *CNN,* November 29, 2011.

7. United States Department of the Treasury, "The Debt to the Penny and Who Holds It," *TreasuryDirect,* http://www.treasurydirect.gov/NP/NPGateway.

8. United States Department of Labor, "Databases, Tables, and Calculators by Subject."

9. Mark J. Perry, "Manufacturing: Employment Falls to Record Lows, But Productivity Soars," December 29, 2009, http://mjperry.blogspot.com/2009/12/manufacturing-employment-falls-to.html.

10. Fareed Zakaria, "How to Restore the American Dream," *Time,* October 21, 2010.

11. Annie Baxter, "Factories 'Reshore' Some Work From Overseas," *NPR News,* March 13, 2012.

12. Zakaria, "How to Restore the American Dream."

13. Teryn Norris, "Asia Challenges US Innovation Leadership, New Report Shows," January 18, 2010, http://leadenergy.org/2010/01/asia-challenges-usa-leadership/.

14. OECD, The OECD Programme for International Student Assessment (PISA), *PISA 2009 Results: Executive Summary,* 8.

15. Yunji de Nies, "President Obama Outlines College Education Goal to Improve College Graduation Rate in the US," ABCNews.com, August 9, 2010.

16. Mary Beth Marklein, "4-year Colleges Graduate 53% of Students in 6 Years," *USA Today,* June 3, 2009.

17. Annalyn Censky, "China: World's Largest Supplier of Educated Works," *CNNMoney,* June 15, 2012.

18. Elizabeth G. Olson, "Confronting the Coming American Worker Shortage," *Fortune,* May 20, 2011.

19. David Jackson, "Obama: Jobs Bill Will Also Improve Education," *USA Today,* September 25, 2011.

20. "United States Public Debt," http://en.wikipedia.org/wiki/United_States_public_debt, (accessed April 15, 2011).

21. US Department of the Treasury, "Debt to the Penny and Who Holds It."

22. Jeanne Sahadi, "Big Deficit for 2011, but Some Improvement on Tap," *CNNMoney,* August 24, 2011.

23. "United States Public Debt."

24. Laurent Belsie, "Growth in a Time of Debt" (April 2010), NBER Digest OnLine, http://www.nber.org/digest/apr10/w15639.html (accessed April 18, 2011).

25. James D. Agresti and Stephen F. Cardone, "Social Security Facts," January 27, 2011 (revised March 4, 2011), http://justfacts.com/socialsecurity.asp.

26. "Medicare (United States)," http://en.wikipedia.org/wiki/Medicare_(United_States) (accessed April 1, 2010).

27. "Post-World War II Baby Boom," http://en.wikipedia.org/wiki/Post-World_War_II_baby_boom (accessed April 1, 2010).

28. "Medicare (United States)."

29. Saundra Young, "Obesity Is Getting Bigger in the United States," CNNHealth, July 7, 2011.

30. United States Department of Health and Human Services, "Childhood Obesity," http://aspe.hhs.gov/health/reports/child_obesity/ (accessed February 4, 2012).

31. Young, "Obesity Is Getting Bigger."

32. United States Social Security and Medicare Boards of Trustees, "Status of the Social Security and Medicare Programs: A Summary of the 2011 Annual Reports."

33. Charles H. Smith, "We're No. 1 (and No. 3)! Surprising Facts about the US and Oil," February 28, 2011, http://www.dailyfinance.com/2011/02/28/surprising-facts-about-us-and-oil/.

34. United States Department of Transportation, Federal Highway Administration, http://www.fhwa.dot.gov/ohim/onh00/bar8.htm (accessed March 25, 2011).

35. "Motor Vehicle Fuel Consumption and Travel in the US, 1960–2006," *Infoplease.com.* http://www.infoplease.com/ipa/A0004727.html (accessed February 4, 2012).

36. "Number of Cars in China Hits 100m," *China Daily,* September 17, 2011.

37. James L. Williams, "Oil Price History and Analysis," http://www.wtrg.com/prices.htm (accessed February 4, 2012).

38. United States Department of Energy, "AEO 2012 Early Release Overview," 4.

39. Zakaria, "How to Restore the American Dream"

CHAPTER 2: THE BENEFITS OF CONFUCIAN INFLUENCE

1. Max Weber, *The Protestant Ethic and the Spirit of Capitalism*, trans. Peter Baehr and Cordon C. Wells (Penguin Books, 2002).

2. "Leibniz on China."

3. Khan, "Confucian Ethic and Economic Growth," 122.

4. MacFarquar, "Post-Confucian Challenge," 68.

5. "Ancient China's Technology," http://east_west_dialogue.tripod.com/id1.html (accessed April 18, 2011).

6. Angus Maddison, "Table B-18. The World GDP, 20 Countries and Regional Total, 0–1998 AD," *The World Economy: A Millennial Perspective,* http://www.theworldeconomy.org/MaddisonTables/MaddisontableB-18.pdf.

7. MacFarquar, "Post-Confucian Challenge," 72.

8. "China GDP Growth."

9. United States Department of Commerce, "Gross Domestic Product, Percent Change From Preceding Period," Bureau of Economic Analysis, 2011, http://www.bea.gov/national/index.htm#gdp (accessed April 20, 2011).

10. "China GDP Growth."

11. Weiming Tu. "The Rise of Industrial East Asia: The Role of Confucian Values," *Modernization Process in East Asia: Economic, Political, and Cultural Perspectives* (Copenhagen Papers on East and Southeast Asian Studies) 36:1 (April 1989), 91.

12. Austin Ramzy, "With Latest Launch, China Plots Course for Space Station," *Time*, September 9, 2011.

13. OECD, *PISA 2009 Results,* 8.

14. Bruce, "China Debuts at Education Rankings."

15. Richard Allen Greene, "China Shoots up Rankings as Science Power, Study Finds," CNN, March 29, 2011.

16. S. Cheryan and G.V. Bodenhausen, "Model Minority," in S. M. Caliendo and C. D. McIlwain, eds., *Routledge Companion to Race and Ethnicity* (Routledge, 2011), 173.

17. Pew Research Center, "Rise of Asian Americans," 1.

18. United States, "Income, Poverty in the United States: 2009."

19. Jochen Kleining, "Dispersed Economic Power? Overseas Chinese between Discrimination and Success in Business," *KAS Overseas Information*, http://www.kas.de/wf/doc/kas_13288-544-2-30.pdf?080402162326 (accessed April 12, 2011).

20. Pew Research Center, "Rise of Asian Americans," 2, 37, 50, 53.

21. United States Department of Education, "ACT Score Averages and Standard Deviations, by Sex and Race/Ethnicity, and Percentage of ACT Test Takers, by Selected Composite Score Ranges and Planned Fields of Study: Selected Years, 1995 through 2010," *Digest of Education Statistics*, National Center for Education Statistics (2011), http://nces.ed.gov/programs/digest/d10/tables/dt10_155.asp

22. United States Department of Education, "SAT Mean Scores of College-bound Seniors, by Race/Ethnicity: Selected Years, 1990/91 through 2009/10," *Digest of Education Statistics,* 2010 (NCES 2011-015), National Center for Education Statistics (2011), http://nces.ed.gov/fastfacts/display.asp?id=171.

23. Rampell, "College Enrollment Rate Record High."

24. Egan, "Challenge Ideas of Race in Universities."

25. Pew Research Center, "Rise of Asian Americans," 65.

26. *A History of Chinese American Achievement in the United States,* directed by Ron Meyer, (New York: Ambrose Video Publishing, Inc., 2009), DVD.

27. "Intel Science Talent Search Winner List (2007–2011)," http://www.intel.com/about/corporateresponsibility/education/sts/winners.htm (accessed February 28, 2012).

28. "Siemens Science Competition Winner List (2007–2011)," http://www.siemens-foundation.org/en/competition.htm (accessed February 28, 2012).

29. *A History of Chinese American Achievement in the United States.*

30. New Century Foundation, "Major Findings," *The Color of Crime: Race, Crime, and Justice in America,* 2005.

31. United States Department of Justice, "Crime in the United States 2008: Arrests by Race," US Federal Bureau of Investigation, Criminal Justice Information Services Division, 2008, http://www2. fbi.gov/ucr/cius2008/data/table_43.html (accessed on April 1, 2011).

32. United States Department of Health and Human Services, "Illicit Drug Use, by Race/Ethnicity, in Metropolitan and Non-Metropolitan Counties: 2004 and 2005," *The NSDUH Report,* June 21, 2007.

33. United States Department of Education, *Status and Trends in the Education of Racial and Ethnic Minorities,* National Center for Educational Statistics, September 2009, 91–105.

34. Terrance J. Reeves and Claudette E. Bettett, "We the People: Asians in the United States" *Census 2000 Special Report,* December 2004, 7

35. United States Department of Health and Human Services, "Obesity and Asian Americans," Office of Minority Health, http:// minorityhealth.hhs.gov/templates/content.aspx?ID=6458   (accessed February 11, 2012).

CHAPTER 3: CONFUCIANISM AND INSPIRING CONFUCIAN VALUES

1. Yutan Lin, *The Wisdom of Confucius,* (New York: The Modern Library, 1994), 54–101.

2. Lin, *The Wisdom of Confucius,* 18–22.

3. Tiantian Song, ed., *Confucian Insightful Words on Life* (Beijing: New World Press, 2008), 127.

4. Yutan Lin, *The Wisdom of Confucius (Chinese Edition)* (Beijing: Qunyuan Press, 2010), 13.

5. Confucius et al., *Four Books & Five Classics* (2009), 86.

6. "Confucianism,"   http://baike.baidu.com/view/40289.htm,   last modified January 13, 2012.

7. Lin, *The Wisdom of Confucius (Chinese Edition),* 9.

8. "Confucianism on Governing by Moral Values," http://wenwen. soso.com/z/q200609107.htm, last modified July 3, 2010.

9. Confucius et al., *Four Books & Five Classics,* ed. Editing Committee of *Superior Collection* (China Pictorial Publishing House, 2011), 239.

10. Lin, *Wisdom of Confucius,* 13–17.

11. Ibid., 235.

12. Wang, Yinglin (王应麟), et al., *Three Word Chant, One Hundred Chinese Surnames, and Essay of One Thousand Words* (Beijing: Huawen Press, 2009), 29–31.

13. Confucius et al., *Four Books & Five Classics* (2009), 45.

14. Lin, *Wisdom of Confucius (Chinese Edition),* 19.

15. Jicheng Shen, "Confucianism on Wisdom," *Wisdom: The Shining Light of Soul for Thousands of Years* (Guilin: People's Press of Guangxi, 2007), 5–6.

16. Confucius et al., *Four Books & Five Classics* (2011), 116.

17. Confucius et al., *Four Books & Five Classics* (2009), 382.

18. Ibid., 99.

19. Lin, *Wisdom of Confucius,* 23–24.

20. Confucius et al., *Four Books & Five Classics* (2009), 3.

21. "Confucianism."

22. "Leibniz on China."

23. "Imperial Examination System," http://baike.baidu.com/view/13684. htm, last modified February 26, 2012.

24. Confucius et al., "Preface," *Four Books & Five Classics* (2009).

25. Wang, "Preface," *Three Word Chant.*

26. Ibid., 15.

CHAPTER 4: FIRST VALUE: LI-ZHI (立志) "DETERMINATION FOR AN OUTSTANDING LIFE"

1. Tommy Tomlinson, *Hard Work and High Expectation: Motivating Students to Learn,* (US Department of Education, 1992), 1–14.

2. Richard Ingersoll and Thomas M. Smith, "The Wrong Solution to the Teacher Shortage," *Education Leadership,* May 2003, 32.

3. Patrick Welsh, "For Once, Blame the Student," *USA Today*, March 7, 2006.
4. Robert J. Samuelson, "School Reform's Meager Results," *Washington Post*, September 6, 2010.
5. L.Z. Granderson, "Parents, Time to Panic about Our Kids' Education," *CNN*, August 23, 2011.
6. Claudio Sanchez and Linda Wertheimer, "School Dropout Rates Add To Fiscal Burden," *NPR News*, July 24, 2011.
7. Anthony P. Carnevale, Stephen J. Rose, and Ban Cheah, "The College Payoff: Education, Occupations, Lifetime Earnings," Georgetown University Center on Education and the Workforce, August 5, 2011, 3.
8. Thomas Friedman, "We are No 1(1)!" *New York Times*, September 1, 2010.
9. Olson, "Confronting American Worker Shortage."
10. Christine Matthews, "Foreign Science and Engineering Presence in US Institutions and the Labor Force," Congressional Research Service, October 28, 2010, 12.
11. Olson, "Confronting American Worker Shortage."
12. Lin, *Wisdom of Confucius (Chinese Edition)*, 60.
13. Confucius et al., *Four Books & Five Classics* (2009), 3.
14. Ibid., 107.
15. Geliang Zhu,"Advice to My Nephew," http://baike.baidu.com/view/677587.htm, last modified December 28, 2011.
16. Confucius et al., *Four Books & Five Classics* (2009), 45.
17. Wang, *Three Word Chant*, 85.
18. http://zhidao.baidu.com/question/332695737.html, last modified October 22, 2011.
19. Shanghai Editing Institute of Chinese Book Bauru, *Chinese Loose-leaf Selections*, Volume 2 (Shanghai Ancient Book Publishing House, 1979,), 180.
20. Song, *Confucian Insightful Words on Life*, 272.
21. Confucius et al., *Four Books & Five Classics* (2009), 75.
22. Wang, *Three Word Chant*, 84–93.

23. *Becoming American: The Chinese Experience,* directed by Bill Moyer (Public Affairs Television, Inc., 2003), videocassette.

24. Pew Research Center, "Rise of Asian Americans," 130.

25. "Elaine L. Chao," http://www.notablebiographies.com/newsmakers2/2007-A-Co/Chao-Elaine-L.html (accessed April 18, 2011).

26. "Becoming American: Interview with Maya Lin," by Bill Moyers, Public Affairs Television, http://www.pbs.org/becomingamerican/ap_pjourneys_transcript5d.html (accessed April 15, 2011).

27. Michelle Kwan, *Heart of a Champion,* (New York: Scholastic, 1997), 18–19.

28. Zheng Chang, "The Story of Lang Lang," http://blog.sina.com.cn/s/blog_4b810dda0100frkp.html (accessed April 15, 2011).

29. Confucius et al., *Four Books & Five Classics* (2009), 381.

30. "Interview with John Sie," by Tom Southwick, *The Hauser Oral and Video History Collection,* http://www.cablecenter.org/content.cfm?id=663 (accessed April 18, 2011).

31. Ibid.

32. Pew Research Center, "Rise of Asian Americans," 139.

33. Kwan, *Heart of a Champion,* 22–27.

34. Pew Research Center, "Rise of Asian Americans," 4.

35. "Ang Lee," http://en.wikipedia.org/wiki/Ang_Lee, last modified August 2009.

36. Kwan, *Heart of a Champion,* 22–27, 56–58, 96–101.

CHAPTER 5: SECOND VALUE: QIN-XUE (勤学) "PURSUING AN EXCELLENT EDUCATION"

1. United States Department of Education, "Secretary Arne Duncan's Remarks at OECD's Release of the Program for International Student Assessment (PISA) 2009 Results," press release, December 7, 2010.

2. United States Department of Labor, "Education Pays," Bureau of Labor Statistics, http://www.bls.gov/emp/ep_chart_001.htm (accessed April 25, 2011).

3. Olson, "Confronting American Worker Shortage."

4. "Confucius and Mencius on Learning," http://baike.baidu.com/view/1483028.htm, last modified March 3, 2012.

5. Wang, *Three Word Chant*, 96.

6. Confucius et al., *Four Books & Five Classics* (2009), 380.

7. Ibid., 381.

8. Ibid., 380.

9. Song, *Confucian Insightful Words on Life*, 14.

10. Confucius et al., *Four Books & Five Classics* (2009), 380.

11. Ibid., 380.

12. Wang, *Three Word Chant*, 81–83.

13. Ibid., 6.

14. Ibid., 5.

15. Ibid., 4.

16. "Becoming American: Interview with David Ho, MD," by Bill Moyers, Public Affairs Television, http://www.pbs.org/becomingamerican/ap_pjourneys_transcript3.html (accessed April 18, 2011).

17. *Becoming American: The Chinese Experience.*

18. "Remarks by the President at White House Science Fair," October 18, 2010, http://www.whitehouse.gov/the-press-office/2010/10/18/remarks-president-white-house-science-fair.

19. Tomlinson, *Motivating Students to Learn*, 2, 7.

20. Mareen Staut, *The Feel-Good Curriculum: The Dumbing Down of America's Kids in the Name of Self-Esteem* (Cambridge: Perseus Publishing, 2001).

21. Samuelson, "School Reform's Meager Results."

22. ACT, "The Condition of College and Career Readiness 2012," 1.

23. Jessica Hopper, "Is China's Education System Keeping Up With Growing Superpower?" *ABC News,* November 16, 2010.

24. Olson, "Confronting American Worker Shortage."

25. Vincent Fernando, "It's Official, Asian-American Students Work Way Harder To Become More Educated Than Everyone Else," *Business Insider,* January 27, 2010, http://www.businessinsider.com/why-do-asian-american-students-try-to-become-more-educated-than-the-rest-2010-1#ixzz1I2o0kVMT.

26. Hopper, "China's Education System."

27. *America: The Story of Us,* produced by NYPTOPIA for History (A&E Television Network, 2010), DVD.

28. Tomlinson, *Motivating Students to Learn,* 7.

29. Welsh, "For Once, Blame the Student."

30. Pew Research Center, "Rise of Asian Americans," 125.

31. Wang, *Three Word Chant,* 6.

32. Marina Ma, *My Son, Yo-Yo,* ed. John A. Rallo, (Hong Kong: The Chinese University Press, 1995), 31–34.

33. Amy Chua, *Battle Hymn of the Tiger Mom* (New York: Penguin, 2011), 1–2.

34. Amanda Ripley, "Teacher, Leave Those Kids Alone," *Time,* September 25, 2011.

35. *Becoming American: The Chinese Experience.*

36. "Andrea Jung," http://www.goldsea.com/WW/Jungandrea/jungandrea. html (accessed April 25, 2011).

37. Assia Boundaoui, "Why Would-be Engineers End up as English Majors," *CNN,* May 20, 2011.

38. Chua, *Battle Hymn of the Tiger Mom,* 70.

39. "Confucius and Mencius on Learning."

CHAPTER 6: THIRD VALUE: *JIE-JIAN* (节俭) "SAVING FOR A BETTER LIFE"

1. Liz Zuliani, "A Dozen Alarming Consumer Debt Statistics," *Money Watch,* May 21, 2011, http://www.economywatch.com/ economy-business-and-finance-news/a-dozen-alarming-consumer-debt-statistics.21-05.html

2. Allan C. Garner, "Should Decline in the Personal Saving Rate Be a Cause for Concern?" Federal Reserve Bank at Kansas City, *Economic Review,* 2nd Quarter 2006.

3. Wells Fargo Retirement Survey, "80 Is The New 65 For Many Middle Class Americans When It Comes To Retirement," November 16, 2011, https://www.wellsfargo.com/press/2011/201111 16_80IsTheNew65.

4. Clark Howard, "Can China Own Us?" *CNN,* May 20, 2009.

5. Xinhua, "2005-2009 Household Saving Balance of Urban and Rural Residents," February 25, 2010, http://news.sohu.com/20100225/n270434217.shtml.

6. Center for Responsible Lending, "Unfair and Unsafe: How Countrywide's Irresponsible Practices Have Harmed Borrowers and Shareholders," *CRL Issue Paper*, February 7, 2008, 4.

7. Sara Murray and Conor Dougherty, "Personal Bankruptcy Filings Rising Fast," *Wall Street Journal*, January 7, 2010.

8. Lynn Adler, "US 2009 Foreclosures Shatter Record Despite Aid," *Reuters*, January 14, 2010.

9. Lin, *Wisdom of Confucius (Chinese Edition)*, 43.

10. Wang Wugang, "Confucianism on Money Management," http://blog.sina.com.cn/s/blog_4cb1287b0100bc9t.html, last modified December 7, 2008.

11. Confucius et al., *Four Books & Five Classics* (2009), 11.

12. "Famous Words on Thrift and Saving (in Chinese)," http://zhidao.baidu.com/question/18925595, last modified February 4, 2007.

13. Shao Difei, et al., *Appreciation Dictionary of Tang Poems*, (Shanghai: Shanghai Dictionary Press, 1983), 916.

14. Wang, "Confucianism on Money Management."

15. Blake Ellis, "Credit Cards from Hell," *CNNMoney*, September 8, 2011.

16. Peter Cohan, "Want to Protest Wall Street's Bonus Bonanza? Good Luck," January 17, 2012, http://www.dailyfinance.com/2010/01/17/want-to-protest-wall-streets-bonus-bonanza-good-luck/.

17. Thomas DiNapoli, "Wall Street Bonuses Rose Sharply in 2009," news release from the Office of New York State Comptroller, February 23, 2010.

18. Confucius et al., *Four Books & Five Classics* (2009), 97.

19. Center for Responsible Lending. "Countrywide's Irresponsible Practices," 4.

CHAPTER 7: FOURTH VALUE: *GU-JIA* (顾家) "CARING FOR YOUR FAMILY"

1. Patrick Fagan and Robert Rector, "The Effects of Divorce on America," June 5, 2000, http://www.heritage.org/research/reports/2000/06/the-effects-of-divorce-on-america

2. Brian Willats, "Breaking Up Is Easy To Do," available from Michigan Family Forum, citing Statistical Abstract of the United States, 1993, 385, http://www.divorcereform.org/econ.html (accessed May 27, 2011).

3. Fagan and Robert Rector, "Effects of Divorce on America."

4. "Annual Causes of Death in the United States," http://drugwarfacts.org/cms/?q=node/30 (accessed February 5, 2012).

5. Wang, *Three Word Chant,* 29–31.

6. D.T.I. Shek and M.F. Lai, "Conceptions of an Ideal Family in Confucian Thoughts: Implication for Individual and Family Counseling," *Asian Journal of Counseling* 7, no. 2 (2000): 85–104.

7. Lin, *Wisdom of Confucius (Chinese edition),* 167.

8. D.T.I. Shek and M.F. Lai, "Conceptions of an Ideal Family in Confucian Thoughts," 85–104.

9. Pew Research Center, "Rise of Asian Americans," 3.

10. Kwan, *Heart of a Champion,* 56–58.

11. Zheng Chang. "Story of Lang Lang."

12. "Amy Chua," http://en.wikipedia.org/wiki/Amy_Chua (accessed March 18, 2012).

13. Yongchun Zhu, Zhitui Yuan, and Su Wang, *Zhu-Zi's Family Teaching, Yuan's Family Teaching, and Family Dialog of Confucius* (Xi'An: San-Qin Press, 2007), 1–9.

14. Reeves, "Asians in the United States," 7.

15. Dongxiao Yang, "Gary Locke: We Have Never Forgot Where We Came From," *View on History,* August 24, 2012, http://blog.sina.com.cn/s/blog_4d77291f0102e0ag.html?tj=1.

16. D.T.I. Shek and M.F. Lai, "Conceptions of an Ideal Family in Confucian Thoughts," 85–104.

17. Wang, *Three Word Chant,* 12.

18. Song, *Confucian Insightful Words on Life*, 136.
19. Lin, *Wisdom of Confucius (Chinese edition)*, 159.
20. Chua, *Battle Hymn of the Tiger Mom*, 52.

CHAPTER 8: FIFTH VALUE: *ZE -YOU* (择友) "DEVELOPING DESIRABLE FRIENDSHIPS"

1. Lev Grossman, "Person of the Year 2010: Mark Zuckerberg," *Time*, December 15, 2010.
2. Janet Kornblum, "Study: 25% of Americans Have No One To Confide In," *USA Today*, June 22, 2006.
3. Wang, *Three Word Chant*, 29–31.
4. Confucius et al., *Four Books & Five Classics* (2009), 97.
5. "Confucian Friendship Guidelines," http://blog.sina.com.cn/s/blog_5c380e9b0100fx41.html, last modified January 13, 2010.
6. Ibid.
7. Ibid.
8. Ibid.
9. Confucius et al., *Four Books & Five Classics* (2009), 99.
10. Ibid., 51.
11. "Confucian Friendship Guidelines."
12. Wang, *Three Word Chant*, 4.
13. Song, ed., *Confucian Insightful Words on Life*, 127.
14. Lin, *The Wisdom of Confucius*, 21.
15. Confucius et al., *Four Books & Five Classics* (2009), 86.
16. Ibid., 60.
17. Lin, *Wisdom of Confucius (Chinese edition)*, 159.
18. "Confucian Friendship Guidelines."
19. Confucius et al., *Four Books & Five Classics* (2009), 380.
20. Brent Schlender, "How a Virtuoso Plays The Web Eclectic, Inquisitive, and Academic, Yahoo's Jerry Yang Reinvents the Role of the Entrepreneur," March 6, 2000, http://money.cnn.com/magazines/fortune/fortune_archive/2000/03/06/275253/index.htm.

Bibliography

A History of Chinese American Achievement in the United States. Directed by Ron Meyer. New York: Ambrose Video Publishing, Inc., 2009. DVD.

ACT, "The Condition of College and Career Readiness 2012."

Adler, Lynn. "US 2009 Foreclosures Shatter Record Despite Aid." *Reuters.* January 14, 2010.

Ahmed, Kamal. "Jim O'Neill: China Could Overtake US Economy by 2027." *Telegraph.* November 19, 2011.

America: The Story of Us. Produced by NYPTOPIA for History. A&E Television Network, 2010.

"Amy Chua." http://en.wikipedia.org/wiki/Amy_Chua (accessed March 18, 2012).

"Ancient China's Technology." http://east_west_dialogue.tripod.com/id1. html (accessed April 18, 2011).

"Ang Lee." http://en.wikipedia.org/wiki/Ang_Lee. Last modified August 2009.

"Annual Causes of Death in the United States." http://drugwarfacts.org/ cms/?q=node/30.

Agresti, James D. and Stephen F. Cardone. "Social Security Facts." January 27, 2011. Revised March 4. 2011. http://justfacts.com/ socialsecurity.asp.

"Andrea Jung." http://www.goldsea.com/WW/Jungandrea/jungandrea.html.

Baxter, Annie. "Factories 'Reshore' Some Work From Overseas." *NPR News.* March 13, 2012.

Becoming American: The Chinese Experience. Directed by Bill Moyers. Public Affairs Television, Inc., 2003.

"Becoming American: Interview with David Ho, MD." By Bill Moyers. Public Affairs Television. http://www.pbs.org/becomingamerican/ap pjourneys transcript3.html.

"Becoming American: Interview with Maya Lin." By Bill Moyers. Public Affairs Television. http://www.pbs.org/becomingamerican/ ap pjourneys transcript5d.html.

Belsie, Laurent. "Growth in a Time of Debt" (April 2010). NBER Digest OnLine. http://www.nber.org/digest/apr10/w15639.html.

Boundaoui, Assia. "Why Would-be Engineers End up as English Majors." *CNN.* May 20, 2011.

Bruce, Mary. "China Debuts at Top of International Education Rankings." *ABCNews.* December 7, 2011.

Carnevale, Anthony P., Stephen J. Rose, and Ban Cheah. *The College Payoff: Education, Occupations, Lifetime Earnings.* Georgetown University Center on Education and the Workforce. August 5, 2011.

Censky, Annalyn. "China: World's Largest Supplier of Educated Works." *CNNMoney.* June 15, 2012.

Center for Responsible Lending. "Unfair and Unsafe: How Countrywide's Irresponsible Practices Have Harmed Borrowers and Shareholders." *CRL Issue Paper.* February 7, 2008.

Chang, Zheng. "The Story of Lang Lang." http://blog.sina.com.cn/s/ blog 4b810dda0100frkp.html.

"China GDP Growth," *Index Mundi.* http://www.indexmundi.com/china/ gdp real growth rate.html (accessed April 30, 2011).

Chua, Amy. *Battle Hymn of the Tiger Mom.* New York: Penguin, 2011.

Cheryan S. and G.V. Bodenhausen. "Model Minority." In *Routledge Companion to Race and Ethnicity,* edited by S. M. Caliendo and C. D. McIlwain. New York: Routledge, 2011.

Cohan, Peter. "Want to Protest Wall Street's Bonus Bonanza? Good Luck." January 17, 2010. http://www.dailyfinance.com/2010/01/17/ want-to-protest-wall-streets-bonus-bonanza-good-luck/.

"Confucian Friendship Guidelines." http://blog.sina.com.cn/s/blog_5c380e9b0100fx41.html. Last modified January 13, 2010.

"Confucianism." http://baike.baidu.com/view/40289.htm. Last modified January 13, 2012.

"Confucianism on Governing by Moral Values." http://wenwen.soso.com/z/q200609107.htm. Last modified July 3, 2010.

"Confucius and Mencius on Learning." http://baike.baidu.com/view/1483028.htm. Last modified March 3, 2012.

Confucius et al. *Four Books & Five Classics.* Edited by Editing Committee of *Superior Collection.* China Pictorial Publishing House, 2011.

Confucius et al. *Four Books & Five Classics.* Edited by Zefei Li. Shenyang: Wanjuan Publishing House, 2009.

"Crude Oil Price History." http://www.nyse.tv/crude-oil-price-history.htm.

de Nies, Yunji. "President Obama Outlines College Education Goal to Improve College Graduation Rate in the US." *ABCNews.com.* August 9, 2010.

Egan, Timothy. "Asian-Americans Challenge Ideas of Race in US Universities." *International Herald Tribune.* January 7, 2007.

"Elaine L. Chao." http://www.notablebiographies.com/newsmakers2/2007-A-Co/Chao-Elaine-L.html.

Ellis, Blake. "Credit Cards from Hell." *CNNMoney.* September 8, 2011.

Fagan, Patrick and Robert Rector. "The Effects of Divorce on America." June 5, 2000. http://www.heritage.org/research/reports/2000/06/the-effects-of-divorce-on-america.

"Famous Words on Thrift and Saving (in Chinese)" http://zhidao.baidu.com/question/18925595. Last modified February 4, 2007.

Fernando, Vincent. "It's Official, Asian-American Students Work Way Harder To Become More Educated Than Everyone Else." *Business Insider.* January 27, 2010. http://www.businessinsider.com/why-do-asian-american-students-try-to-become-more-educated-than-the-rest-2010-1#ixzz1I2o0kVMT.

Friedman, Thomas. "We are No 1(1)!" *New York Times.* September 1, 2010.

Garner, Allan C. "Should Decline in the Personal Saving Rate Be a Cause for Concern?" Federal Reserve Bank at Kansas City. *Economic Review.* 2nd Quarter 2006.

Ghosh, Palash R. "Asian-Americans Endure Well During Recession, But 'Model Minority' Theory Has Some Holes in It." *International Business Times.* July 29, 2010.

Granderson, L.Z. "Parents, Time to Panic about Our Kids' Education." *CNN.* August 23, 2011.

Greene, Richard Allen. "China Shoots up Rankings as Science Power, Study Finds." *CNN.* March 29, 2011.

Gregory, Anthony. "What Price War: Afghanistan, Iraq, and the Costs of Conflict." The Independent Institute. June 2011.

Grossman, Lev. "Person of the Year 2010: Mark Zuckerberg." *Time.* December 15, 2010.

Hopper, Jessica. "Is China's Education System Keeping Up With Growing Superpower?" *ABC News.* November 16, 2010.

Howard, Clark. "Can China Own Us?" *CNN.* May 20, 2009.

Howell, George and Kyle Almond. "Many American Families Running on Financial Fumes." *CNN.* November 29, 2011.

"Imperial Examination System." http://baike.baidu.com/view/13684.htm. Last modified February 26, 2012.

Ingersoll, Richard and Thomas M. Smith. "The Wrong Solution to the Teacher Shortage." *Education Leadership.* May 2003.

"Intel Science Talent Search Winner List (2007-2011)." Accessed on February 28, 2012. http://www.intel.com/about/corporateresponsibility/education/sts/winners.htm.

Jackson, David. "Obama: Jobs Bill Will Also Improve Education." *USA Today.* September 25, 2011.

Kahn, Herman. "The Confucian Ethic and Economic Growth." In *World Economic Development: 1979 and Beyond.* Westview, 1979.

Kleining, Jochen. "Dispersed Economic Power? Overseas Chinese between Discrimination and Success in Business." *KAS Overseas Information.* http://www.kas.de/wf/doc/kas_13288-544-2-30.pdf?080402162326.

Kornblum, Janet. "Study: 25% of Americans Have No One To Confide In." *USA Today.* June 22, 2006.

Kwan, Michelle. *Heart of a Champion.* New York: Scholastic, 1997.

"Leibniz on China, from the Preface to the Novissima Sinica (1697/1699)." http://east_west_dialogue.tripod.com/id12.html.

Lin, Yutan. *The Wisdom of Confucius (Chinese Edition).* Beijing: Qunyuan Press, 2010.

Lin, Yutan. *The Wisdom of Confucius.* New York: The Modern Library, 1994.

Ma, Marina. *My Son, Yo-Yo.* Edited by John A. Rallo. Hong Kong: The Chinese University Press, 1995.

Marklein, Mary Beth. "4-year Colleges Graduate 53% of Students in 6 Years." *USA Today.* June 3, 2009.

MacFarquar, Roderick. "The Post-Confucian Challenge," *The Economist.* February 9, 1980, 67-72.

Maddison, Angus. "Table B-18. The World GDP, 20 Countries and Regional Total, 0-1998 AD" *The World Economy: A Millennial Perspective.* http://www.theworldeconomy.org/MaddisonTables/MaddisontableB-18.pdf.

Matthews, Christine. "Foreign Science and Engineering Presence in US Institutions and the Labor Force." Congressional Research Service. October 28, 2010.

"Medicare (United States)." http://en.wikipedia.org/wiki/Medicare_(United_States).

"Motor Vehicle Fuel Consumption and Travel in the US, 1960–2006." *Infoplease.com.* http://www.infoplease.com/ipa/A0004727.html.

Murray, Sara and Conor Dougherty. "Personal Bankruptcy Filings Rising Fast." *Wall Street Journal.* January 7, 2010.

New Century Foundation. "Major Findings." *The Color of Crime: Race, Crime, and Justice in America.* 2005.

Norris, Teryn. "Asia Challenges US Innovation Leadership, New Report Shows." January 18, 2010. http://leadenergy.org/2010/01/asia-challenges-usa-leadership/.

"Number of Cars in China Hits 100m." *China Daily.* September 17, 2011.

OECD. The OECD Programme for International Student Assessment (PISA). *PISA 2009 Results: Executive Summary.* 2010. http://www.oecd.org/dataoecd/34/60/46619703.pdf.

Olson, Elizabeth G. "Confronting the Coming American Worker Shortage." *Fortune.* May 20, 2011.

Perry, Mark J. "Manufacturing: Employment Falls to Record Lows, But Productivity Soars." December 29, 2009. http://mjperry.blogspot.com/2009/12/manufacturing-employment-falls-to.html.

Pew Research Center. "The Rise of Asian Americans." June 19, 2012.

"Post-World War II Baby Boom." http://en.wikipedia.org/wiki/Post-World_War_II_baby_boom.

Rampell, Catherine. "College Enrollment Rate at Record High." *The New York Times.* April 28, 2010.

Ramzy, Austin. "With Latest Launch, China Plots Course for Space Station." *Time.* September 9, 2011.

RealtyTrac Staff. "Record 2.9 Million US Properties Receive Foreclosure Filings in 2010 Despite 30-Month Low in December." January 13, 2011. http://www.realtytrac.com/content/foreclosure-market-report/record-29-million-us-properties-receive-foreclosure-filings-in-2010-despite-30-month-low-in-december-6309.

Reeves, Terrance J. and Claudette E. Bettett. "We the People: Asians in the United States." *Census 2000 Special Report.* December 2004.

"Remarks by the President at White House Science Fair." October 18, 2010. http://www.whitehouse.gov/the-press-office/2010/10/18/remarks-president-white-house-science-fair.

Ripley, Amanda. "Teacher, Leave Those Kids Alone." *Time.* September 25, 2011.

Sahadi, Jeanne. "Big Deficit for 2011, but Some Improvement on Tap." *CNNMoney.* August 24, 2011.

Samuelson, Robert J. "School Reform's Meager Results." *Washington Post.* September 6, 2010.

Sanchez, Claudio and Linda Wertheimer. "School Dropout Rates Add To Fiscal Burden." *NPR News.* July 24, 2011.

Schlender, Brent. "How a Virtuoso Plays the Web Eclectic, Inquisitive, and Academic, Yahoo's Jerry Yang Reinvents the Role of the

Entrepreneur." March 6, 2000. http://money.cnn.com/magazines/fortune/fortune_archive/2000/03/06/275253/index.htm.

Shanghai Editing Institute of Chinese Book Bauru, *Chinese Loose-leaf Selections,* Volume 2. Shanghai: Shanghai Ancient Book Publishing House, 1979.

Shao, Difei, et al. *Appreciation Dictionary of Tang Poems.* Shanghai: Shanghai Dictionary Press, 1983.

Shek, D.T.I. and M.F. Lai. "Conceptions of an Ideal Family in Confucian Thoughts: Implication for Individual and Family Counseling." *Asian Journal of Counseling7,* no. 2 (2000), 85-104. http://money.cnn.com/2011/08/24/news/economy/federal_budget_cbo/index.htm.

Shen, Jicheng. "Confucianism on Wisdom." *Wisdom: The Shining Light of Soul for Thousands of Years.* Guilin: People's Press of Guangxi, 2007.

"Siemens Science Competition Winner List (2007-2011)." http://www.siemens-foundation.org/en/competition.htm.

Smith, Charles H. "We're No. 1 (and No. 3)! Surprising Facts about the US and Oil." February 28, 2011. http://www.dailyfinance.com/2011/02/28/surprising-facts-about-us-and-oil/.

Song, Tiantian, ed. *Confucian Insightful Words on Life.* Beijing: New World Press, 2008.

Southwick, Tom. "Interview with John Sie," *The Hauser Oral and Video History Collection.* http://www.cablecenter.org/content.cfm?id=663.

Stout, Maureen. *The Feel-Good Curriculum: The Dumbing-Down of America's Kids in the Name of Self-Esteem.* Cambridge: Perseus Publishing, 2000.

Tomlinson, Tommy. *Hard Work and High Expectation: Motivating Students to Learn.* US Department of Education, 1992.

Tu, Weiming. "The Rise of Industrial East Asia: The Role of Confucian Values." *Modernization Process in East Asia: Economic, Political, and Cultural Perspectives* (Copenhagen Papers on East and Southeast Asian Studies) 36:1 (April 1989).

United States Bureau of Labor Statistics. "The 2010 Census: The Employment Impact of Counting the Nation." *Monthly Labor Review.* March 2011.

United States Department of Commerce. "Gross Domestic Product, Percent Change from Preceding Period." Bureau of Economic Analysis. 2011. http://www.bea.gov/national/index.htm#gdp.

United States Department of Commerce. "Income, Poverty, and Health Insurance Coverage in the United States: 2009." *US Census Bureau Current Population Reports.* September 2010.

United States Department of Education. "ACT Score Averages and Standard Deviations, by Sex and Race/Ethnicity, and Percentage of ACT Test Takers, by Selected Composite Score Ranges and Planned Fields of Study: Selected Years, 1995 through 2010." *Digest of Education Statistics.* National Center for Education Statistics (2011). http://nces.ed.gov/programs/digest/d10/tables/dt10_155.asp.

United States Department of Education. "SAT Mean Scores of College-bound Seniors, By Race/Ethnicity: Selected Years, 1990/91 Through 2009/10" (NCES 2011-015). *Digest of Education Statistics.* National Center for Education Statistics (2011). http://nces.ed.gov/fastfacts/display.asp?id=171.

United States Department of Education. "Secretary Arne Duncan's Remarks at OECD's Release of the Program for International Student Assessment (PISA) 2009 Results." Press release. December 7, 2010.

United States Department of Education. *Status and Trends in the Education of Racial and Ethnic Minorities.* National Center for Educational Statistics. September 2009.

United States Department of Energy. "AEO 2012 Early Release Overview."

United States Department of Health and Human Services. "Childhood Obesity." http://aspe.hhs.gov/health/reports/child_obesity/.

United States Department of Health and Human Services. "Illicit Drug Use, by Race/Ethnicity, in Metropolitan and Non-Metropolitan Counties: 2004 and 2005." *The NSDUH Report.* June 21, 2007.

United States Department of Health and Human Services, "Obesity and Asian Americans." Office of Minority Health. http://minorityhealth.hhs.gov/templates/content.aspx?ID=6458 Accessed February 11, 2012.

United States Department of Justice. "Crime in the United States 2008: Arrests by Race." US Federal Bureau of Investigation, Criminal Justice Information Services Division. 2008. http://www2.fbi.gov/ucr/cius2008/data/table_43.html. Accessed April 1, 2011.

United States Department of Labor. Bureau of Labor Statistics. "Databases, Tables, and Calculators by Subject." http://data.bls.gov/cgi-bin/surveymost.

United States Department of Transportation—Federal Highway Administration. http://www.fhwa.dot.gov/ohim/onh00/bar8.htm.

United States Department of the Treasury. "The Debt to the Penny and Who Holds It." *TreasuryDirect.* http://www.treasurydirect.gov/NP/NPGateway.

"United States Public Debt." http://en.wikipedia.org/wiki/United_States_public_debt.

United States Social Security and Medicare Boards of Trustees. "Status of the Social Security and Medicare Programs: A Summary of the 2011 Annual Reports."

Wang, Wugang. "Confucianism on Money Management." http://blog.sina.com.cn/s/blog_4cb1287b0100bc9t.html. Last modified December 7, 2008.

Wang, Yinglin (王应麟), et al. *Three Word Chant, One Hundred Chinese Surnames, and Essay of One Thousand Words.* Beijing: Huawen Press, 2009.

Weber, Max. *The Protestant Ethic and the Spirit of Capitalism.* Translated by Peter Baehr and Cordon C. Wells. Penguin, 2002.

Wells Fargo Retirement Survey. "80 Is The New 65 For Many Middle Class Americans When It Comes To Retirement." November 16, 2011. https://www.wellsfargo.com/press/2011/20111116_80IsTheNew65.

Welsh, Patrick "For Once, Blame the Student." *USA Today.* March 7, 2006.

Willats, Brian. "Breaking Up Is Easy To Do." Michigan Family Forum, citing *Statistical Abstract of the United States*, 1993. http://www.divorcereform.org/econ.html.

Williams, James L. "Oil Price History and Analysis." http://www.wtrg.com/prices.htm.

Xinhua, "2005-2009 Household Saving Balance of Urban and Rural Residents." February 25, 2010. http://news.sohu.com/20100225/n270434217.shtml.

Yang, Dongxiao. "Gary Locke: We Have Never Forgot Where We Came From." *View on History*. August 24, 2012. http://blog.sina.com.cn/s/blog_4d77291f0102e0ag.html?tj=1.

Young, Saundra. "Obesity Is Getting Bigger in the United States." *CNNHealth*. July 7, 2011. http://thechart.blogs.cnn.com/2011/07/07/obesity-is-getting-bigger-in-the-united-states/.

Zakaria, Fareed. "How to Restore the American Dream." *Time*. October 21, 2010. http://www.time.com/time/magazine/article/0,9171,2026916,00.html.

Zhu, Geliang. "Advice to My Nephew." http://baike.baidu.com/view/677587.htm. Last modified December 28, 2011.

Zhu, Yongchun, Zhitui Yuan, and Su Wang. *Zhu-Zi's Family Teaching, Yuan's Family Teaching, and Family Dialog of Confucius*. Xi'An: San-Qin Press, 2007.

Zuliani, Liz. "A Dozen Alarming Consumer Debt Statistics." May 21, 2011. *Money Watch*. http://www.economywatch.com/economy-business-and-finance-news/a-dozen-alarming-consumer-debt-statistics.21-05.html.

Index